Almost Meatless

Almost Meatless

Recipes That Are Better for Your Health and the Planet

JOY MANNING and
TARA MATARAZA DESMOND

Photography by Leo Gong

TEN SPEED PRESS
Berkeley | Toronto

....

Ten Speed Press
PO Box 7123
Berkeley, California 94707
www.tenspeed.com

Distributed in Australia by Simon and Schuster Australia, in Canada by Ten Speed Press Canada, in New Zealand by Southern Publishers Group, in South Africa by Real Books, and in the United Kingdom and Europe by Publishers Group UK.

Design by Toni Tajima
Photography by Leo Gong
Food styling by Karen Shinto
Food styling assistance by Jeffrey Larsen
Prop styling by Harumi

Library of Congress Cataloging-in-Publication Data
Manning, Joy.
  Almost meatless : recipes that are better for your health and the planet / Joy Manning and Tara Mataraza Desmond ; photography by Leo Gong.
      p. cm.
  Includes bibliographical references and index.
  Summary: "A collection of sixty-plus recipes that deemphasize the use of meat, with tips for buying quality beef, poultry, fish, and more on a budget and cooking with them healthfully"—Provided by publisher.
  ISBN-13: 978-1-58008-961-6
  ISBN-10: 1-58008-961-5
 1. Cookery (Meat) 2. Cookery, International. I. Desmond, Tara Mataraza. II. Title.
  TX749.M255 2009
  641.6'6—dc22
                          2008037797

Printed in China
First printing this edition, 2009

1 2 3 4 5 6 7 8 9 10 — 13 12 11 10 09

contents

acknowledgments

Tara thanks:

Topher, for countless good things and a very happy life, even in our tiny kitchen; my parents for making our family's dinner table one of the most appetizing, comfortable, inspiring, and supportive places on earth; Marie Simmons for her encouragement and for introducing me to Andy Schloss, who patiently and honestly showed me the ropes; and John and Jen Mataraza, Martha and John Desmond, and Matt and Lis Desmond for being enthusiastic personal publicists of this project.

Joy thanks:

Dan, my dining companion, sous chef, copy editor, taster, tester, researcher, and husband extraordinaire; my dad, Joseph Manning, who drove his carless daughter on countless grocery runs, and my mom, Judy Manning, who has talked this book up for three years; my sister, Jill Manning, and my brother-in-law, Mike Mergen, who never doubted this book would become a reality.

We both thank:

Clare Pelino, our determined agent, for her candid direction, enthusiasm, and steadfast support of the two of us and this project.

Lorena Jones and Ten Speed Press for taking a chance on new authors.

Brie Mazurek for answering our many questions and providing insight and direction.

Very special and endless thanks to our unfailing, dedicated testers—Paula and John Mataraza, Liz Tarpy, and Denise and Kevin Downing—who went above and beyond to help ensure that the recipes in this book are accurate and delicious.

And our trusted tasters, including Dan Call, Topher Desmond, Joseph Manning, Erika and Deacon Chapin, Alicia Steiling, Chris Soltis, Amanda and Gary Schwinn, Allyson Evans, Sarah Schmalbach, and Samantha Bednarek.

introduction

Unlike most vegetarians, I didn't make a conscious decision to live a meat-free lifestyle. I was a fussy eater as a kid, and it was meat-heavy dishes that seemed to gross me out most often. And looking back, it's obvious to me why I picked the ground beef off every Hamburger Helper noodle I ate: it was disgusting. My family's standard dinner fare offered a boneless, skinless chicken breast spritzed with cooking spray and baked at 400°F for around an hour. It wasn't about the environment or animal rights for me when I was a teenager; it was about taste. It seemed to me that meat never tasted good, at least not around my house.

I got more philosophical about my dietary choices during college. The mystery meat within the cafeteria steam trays turned many of my classmates into de facto vegetarians right before my eyes. I met other students (many raised by hippie parents) who preached that a meatless diet was better for the eater, kinder to our fellow living beings, and easier on the earth's resources.

This position made a lot of sense to me. Gradually, I began moving toward a vegan diet, eliminating eggs, cheese, and milk as well. But I dreamed of omelets, and I gained weight because I was subsisting on french fries and falafel. My freezer was stacked with green boxes of manufactured vegetarian "meals."

Ultimately, I left veganism behind at two o'clock in the morning. My father had befriended a neighbor who raised a few chickens in her yard, and he had been bringing home the eggs. The yolks were vibrant and sunny and appetizing; the siren song of their nutrition broke my resolve, which, in light of those happy chickens, didn't make sense to me anymore. There had to be another way of eating that was natural, nutritious, sustainable, and delicious. And it had to include fresh eggs.

During my struggles with the ethics of eating, I became a food writer. For years I had been obsessively studying cookbooks, food magazines, and every chef on PBS and Food Network. I loved to cook, eat, read, write, and think about food. And the more I learned the more apparent it became to me that I wasn't helping anyone, least of all myself, by eating those texturized vegetable protein pucks in my freezer no matter how much *duxelles* I cooked up and smeared on top of them.

For me, the path to my current approach to cooking, which de-emphasizes meat while still embracing it for the flavor it can bring to a balanced meal, started in the restaurants of chefs I believed in. I trusted that the foods would not be overcooked. I trusted that their chickens were farm raised. But like so many people who end up eating in restaurants a lot because of their jobs, I would rather cook at home more often. So I started to take a flexible approach to some of my favorite vegetarian meals, adding just a little bit of meat to dishes to make them taste more like the food I ate at restaurants. Nothing over the top, no steaks or pork chops, nothing that would qualify as Atkins, but a little bacon here, a little chicken there. My husband, a lifelong omnivore, likes his lentil burgers a lot better with bacon on them, and I admit: so do I.

When I approached Tara, this book's coauthor, with my idea for a cookbook, she had never been—and had never considered becoming—a vegetarian. But as a cook and a food writer, she, too, had been thinking a lot about sustainability and what it means to be thoughtful and compassionate about meat consumption. We both recognized you don't have to be a culinary professional to be concerned about these issues. More than ever before, people in all walks of life are talking about what they eat and why.

This book is meant for everyone who wants a delicious and balanced diet. Throughout these chapters, you'll be formally introduced to the most common types of meat, and we will explain what you should seek out, how you can get your hands on it, and why it's worth the trouble.

For example, cattle farmers actually market corn-fed beef like it's a good thing. The reality is that cows can't properly digest corn; they're anatomically equipped to thrive on grass. And while corn does make cows fat faster, it also makes them sick, creating the need for regular doses of antibiotics in their feed.

You don't need to be a nutritionist or an environmental scientist to know that this is bad news. Luckily, it's not all that hard to find a natural, wholesome alternative. All around the country, farmers' markets are offering grass-fed organic beef for your guilt-free enjoyment. Even if you don't have access to a market like that, the Internet provides a wealth of information and mail-order sources for all the ingredients mentioned in this book. We'll show you where to look.

Even the most environment and health conscious among us don't have to restrict our diets anymore. With careful shopping and these recipes, you can do a good deed just by supporting the purveyors who are responsible about their businesses while withholding your dollars from agribusiness. This book is also a resource for those who know they should cut back on the meat in their diets, especially factory-farmed meat, but aren't sure where to start. These practical tips and recipes will point you in the right direction. Before you know it, you may be adapting your family favorites to include more vegetables and grains and less meat.

Though Tara may still be skeptical about the use of tofu and I persist in my doubts about cooking with ground beef, we understand the urgent importance of eating responsibly, regardless of what specific things you choose to eat. Our mission in these pages is to provide a manual for commonsense moderation in the modern American meal.

If you're skeptical that a few ounces of meat are enough to make a dish satisfying and filling, cook our Beefed-Up Bean Chili (page 85). To us, it tastes better than a double cheeseburger. Throughout the book, you'll notice that many of the recipes can be made meatless with a few minor alterations. The flavor won't be the same, but the resulting dishes have tasty personalities of their own and offer meat-free options for when vegetarian company calls or you just want something even lighter.

Enjoy!

—Joy

. . . .

I've never been (and don't plan on becoming) a vegetarian. I grew up with meat, and I like it. The aroma of London broil and baked potatoes from the oven harkens back to weeknight dinners around the table with my family, when I was a kid. Today, one of the most delicious things I know is my mom's beef braciole and the rich tomato sauce it braises in, destined for a dunk from a hunk of crusty, soft Italian bread.

While my mouth waters for pork tenderloin, and I'll happily opt for thinly sliced Genoa salami on my pizza, I am just as hungry for non-meat ingredients. Culinary school, restaurant kitchens, food television, and cookbook recipe development have changed my perspective on techniques and flavor combinations, and have broadened the palette of possibilities. Night after night of the traditional American dinner—with a big piece of meat at the center of the plate—seems a waste of the terrific potential of so many other foods.

The rest of the world is way ahead of us in terms of incorporating smaller amounts of meat as a supporting player in a complete dish. In addition to achieving that balance, other cultures are also better at putting their money where their mouths are. Americans spend a smaller percentage of annual income on food than any other country in the world. We have access to a bounty of fresh, healthful whole foods from our own country's farms, but we put most of our food dollars toward bulk-quantity processed items.

Some of our favorite authors and journalists have been hard at work shedding light on the changing landscape of American farms, the impact of agribusiness, and the state of our health as it relates to what we eat. Their research and reports have given us something to chew on and talk about over our dinner plates, challenging us to rewrite our menus by reconsidering choices—a responsibility that goes far beyond the pantries, stoves, and take-out windows that dot our hectic lives.

As Joy and I researched, wrote, tasted, and talked about this topic, we discovered a growing audience of people who declare themselves omnivores but who have begun to

A Bit of Chicken

Chicken is a dinnertime staple, prized for its versatility and ability to complement other ingredients.

The average American eats 80 pounds of chicken a year. That's substantially more than the roughly 65 pounds of beef and 60 pounds of pork we also consume. For decades, people ate around the same of amount of beef and chicken, but during the past 25 years, as the media began to report extensively on the obesity epidemic and other health risks associated with the consumption of red meat and saturated fats, shoppers became more and more inclined to choose boneless, skinless chicken breasts.

But the way we eat chicken isn't always healthful. Fried chicken, the most commonly enjoyed kind in the United States, certainly doesn't help reduce cholesterol. Replacing beef with chicken works only if you eschew the fried stuff and choose the leanest (and least flavorful) chicken options. And those lean and mean recipes, based on poached boneless, skinless chicken breasts, offer little culinary excitement. Blah meals don't benefit your health if you don't eat them.

There's another way to think about and cook with chicken. Instead of focusing on the fat grams in every portion, cut back significantly on the total amount of chicken you eat. We strongly recommend against ordering chicken at a restaurant, where it is almost surely from a factory-farmed bird. It's easy to enjoy homemade, high-quality chicken dishes with these recipes.

Chicken marries wonderfully with a wide variety of flavorful vegetables and grains. Meals that offer different flavors and textures can be extremely healthful and much more enjoyable than a slab of bland white meat. Starting with a whole chicken is a secret weapon in the battle for big flavor. Chicken bones, rich in gelatin, add depth and body to dishes. Skin creates fond (the foundation of a great soup, stew, or sauce), lends a satisfying layer of flavor, and protects delicate white meat from the direct heat of cooking. It's also easy to discard before the dish is served.

Finally, we want to encourage you to seek out the best chicken you can find. In Philadelphia, where we live, we have terrific farmers' markets, where you can get truly free-range, organic birds directly from the farmer who raises them. Wherever you shop, don't be afraid to grill management on the provenance of the chickens. Today's commercial poultry industry, exempted from the USDA's humane slaughter act because chickens are not legally considered livestock, raises birds in generally abhorrent conditions. Taglines like "all natural" and "free range" have become all but meaningless in the market. The designation "free range" now simply means that chickens have some limited and often unused access to the outdoors. You can look for the "certified humane" label that goes on some products that conform to the Certified Humane Raised & Handled program's standards.

The reality is that these better chickens are much more expensive—sometimes more than twice as expensive—than their factory-farmed counterparts. But the cost reflects the farmers' own expenses. They forgo the cheap corn-based, chemical-laced feed that fattens the birds in a matter of weeks in favor of more natural methods. Savvy shoppers pay premium prices for farm-raised, organic birds, but they get chicken chock-full of robust flavor. You can maximize your investment by learning how to get more flavor from less chicken, how to cut a whole chicken into parts, how to freeze poultry for later use, and how to use the bones to make flavorful stock (page 131).

FREEZE!

For most Americans, eating less meat is going to take some behavior modification. In fact, early on in the recipe development process, a few of our testers confessed to "using the whole package" of sausage or staring at the other half pound of ground beef, unsure of what to do. Obviously, piling on extra sausage links or throwing away perfectly good ground beef is contrary to the ideas in this book.

What's the alternative? While fresh meats may offer slightly better flavor and texture, especially according to food snobs, most cuts of meat and many delicious recipes (like our Roasted Pork Shoulder, page 64, and our Beefed-Up Bean Chili, page 85) freeze exceptionally well. In fact, even your foodie friends probably can't tell the difference.

On a molecular level, ice crystals—formed by freezing—puncture the cells in meat fibers, draining them of their moisture upon thawing and making them slightly tough. Careful freezing and thawing can dramatically minimize these effects. And when you consider the health hazards posed by the meat-rich diet of many Americans, it's a compromise we can live with. Beef lasts longest in the freezer, about a year, while poultry, pork, and fish should be used within three months for best flavor and texture.

It's very important to consider your own convenience when preparing items for the chill chest. Portion your meat (cooked or raw) in recipe-friendly amounts. We suggest freezing individually wrapped chicken breasts, thighs, sausage links, lamb shanks, and steaks. It's best to braise larger cuts (like pork shoulder, lamb shoulder, beef brisket, etc.) that require low-and-slow cooking before stashing and freezing the finished product in 2-cup containers.

We urge you to embrace your freezer. It is one of the best tools you have to use less, preserve more, and extend your dollar, especially when you are paying a premium for top-quality products.

Asian Lettuce Wraps

These wraps are the perfect appetizer for a small, casual dinner party or an exotic entrée for two or four. Dark meat chicken thighs won't dry out in the high heat of the wok, and they take on the intense flavors of this recipe's homemade marinade and stir-fry sauce. What's more, the recipe can just as easily become a salad. By tearing up the lettuce leaves and tossing them with the slaw, you'll make a crunchy, cool bed of greens for the chicken and peanut toppings. **Serves 4**

Chicken

1 teaspoon fish sauce

1 tablespoon soy sauce

1 tablespoon rice wine vinegar

2 tablespoons orange juice

2 tablespoons plus 2 teaspoons vegetable oil

1 (2-inch) piece fresh ginger, peeled and minced (about 1 tablespoon)

2 cloves garlic, minced (about 1 tablespoon)

1/4 teaspoon dried chile flakes

1 scallion, green and white parts, sliced

8 to 12 ounces boneless, skinless chicken thighs (about 4 thighs, or 2 thighs and 2 legs), cut into small cubes or strips

Slaw

3 tablespoons rice wine vinegar

2 tablespoons orange juice

1/4 teaspoon dark (Asian) sesame oil

1/2 teaspoon salt

1/4 teaspoon grated fresh ginger

1 thick carrot (about 4 ounces), cut into 1/8-inch strips

1 cucumber, cut into 1/8-inch strips

2 stalks celery, sliced 1/4 inch thick diagonally

2 to 3 scallions, white and green parts, sliced on the diagonal

16 lettuce leaves (romaine, Boston, Bibb, or green or red leaf)

2 tablespoons roasted salted peanuts, coarsely chopped

TO MARINATE THE CHICKEN, make a marinade by combining the fish sauce, soy sauce, vinegar, orange juice, the 2 tablespoons oil, the ginger, garlic, chile flakes, and scallion in a medium bowl. Add the chicken and stir to coat the meat. Cover the bowl and place in the refrigerator, letting the chicken marinate for at least 30 minutes.

Meanwhile, **TO PREPARE THE SLAW**, whisk together the vinegar, orange juice, sesame oil, salt, and ginger in a large bowl. Toss the vinaigrette together with the carrot, cucumber, celery, and scallions. Taste for seasoning and adjust as needed.

TO PREPARE THE LETTUCE, rinse and pat the leaves dry. Transfer to the refrigerator until ready to use. (If you choose romaine, use the leafy top part of the lettuce for the wrappers. You can tear off the stiffer bottom stem half, chop it up, and add it to the slaw for extra crunch if you like.)

TO COOK THE CHICKEN, heat the 2 teaspoons oil in a large skillet or wok over medium-high heat. Add the marinated chicken and marinade and cook for 5 to 7 minutes, stirring often, until firm to the touch and beginning to brown. Stir in the peanuts.

TO ASSEMBLE AND SERVE, set out the slaw and chicken in bowls along with a platter of the lettuce. Wrap a scoop of slaw and chicken in each lettuce leaf. Have a napkin handy!

Buttermilk Chicken and Portobello Salad

It's no secret that a big bowl of crisp, leafy greens and colorful accompaniments can be a perfectly pleasing meal. But this salad offers meaty sustenance with smoky grill flavors and a tangy herb dressing. A buttermilk marinade tenderizes the lean chicken breasts, and the open flames impart a savory grilled flavor to the antioxidant-packed portobello mushrooms. Bone-in, skin-on chicken pieces can withstand the high heat of the grill and still emerge juicy and flavorful. **Serves 4**

1 cup buttermilk

2 cloves garlic, minced (about 1 tablespoon)

Zest of 1 lemon

1 tablespoon chopped fresh thyme leaves (from about 6 sprigs)

1 tablespoon chopped shallot

Kosher salt and freshly ground black pepper

1 bone-in, skin-on whole chicken breast, split in half

3 portobello mushroom caps

4 (1-inch-thick) slices sourdough or ciabatta bread

1 tablespoon olive oil

Buttermilk Herb Dressing

1/2 cup buttermilk

2 teaspoons canola oil

2 tablespoons freshly squeezed lemon juice

1 tablespoon chopped fresh chives

Leaves from 1 sprig thyme

1/4 cup loosely packed fresh parsley leaves

1/2 clove garlic, minced to a paste

1/4 teaspoon salt

Several grinds black pepper

10 ounces romaine lettuce

1/2 cup crumbled feta cheese

2 tomatoes, cubed

TO MARINATE THE CHICKEN, whisk together the buttermilk, garlic, zest, thyme, shallot, 1 teaspoon salt, and 1/4 teaspoon pepper in a large bowl. Add the chicken, cover, refrigerate, and marinate for at least 1 hour or overnight.

TO GRILL THE CHICKEN, preheat the grill to medium-high and oil the grates. Remove the chicken from the marinade and place on the oiled grates of the hot grill, skin side down. Discard the marinade. Cook for 20 minutes, or until an instant-read thermometer registers 160°F, turning once or twice.

Meanwhile, brush the mushroom caps and bread slices with the oil. Sprinkle the mushrooms with salt and pepper. Add the mushrooms to the grill, cooking for a total of about 8 minutes, flipping once. Add the bread slices and toast for 3 minutes on both sides, or just until grill marks appear. Remove the chicken, mushrooms, and bread and let cool before slicing. Cut the chicken off the bone and slice the meat and mushrooms into 1/4-inch pieces. Cut the bread into large cubes.

TO MAKE THE DRESSING, put the buttermilk, oil, lemon juice, chives, thyme, parsley, garlic, salt, and pepper in a blender and pulse several times until smooth and creamy. Taste for seasoning and adjust as needed.

TO ASSEMBLE THE SALAD, toss the lettuce, cheese, and tomatoes with the dressing in a large bowl. Top the salad with chicken, mushrooms, and grilled bread croutons.

FAKING FAST FOOD: **FIVE TIPS FOR ROTISSERIE CHICKEN**

We would never suggest you forgo home roasting in favor of one of the many supermarket options for rotisserie chicken. What we do suggest is that you consider a rotisserie bird an alternative to the drive-through window. Here are five superfast options to put dinner on the table without a fuss:

1. Shred chicken, arrange over prewashed salad greens, drizzle with olive oil and lemon juice, and scatter over the top whatever cheese you have on hand. We like crumbly blues.

2. Boil a tiny pasta shape, like riso, in chicken stock (page 131) instead of water. Stir in chunks of chicken, a flurry of Parmesan, and a squeeze of lemon juice for a comforting, instant soup. A sprinkle of fresh parsley, if it's on hand, lends freshness.

3. Warm corn tortillas in the toaster oven. Shred chicken and warm up a can of vegetarian refried beans for a taco filling. Top with your favorite jarred salsa.

4. Spread a thin layer of leftover rice on top of a 10-inch tortilla or wrap. Create a line of chicken chunks, as though you're making a sushi roll, and place a line of jarred red pepper strips next to it. Roll and slice like sushi.

5. Stem a portobello mushroom cap and brush the underside with oil. Top with a tablespoon of tomato sauce, chicken chunks, and mozzarella and bake for 10 minutes in a 400°F oven for a heart-healthy take on pizza.

Chicken and Curried Cauliflower Salad Sandwiches

Chicken salad can be boring. Our version adds bold spices and crunchy nuts to the sometimes bland sandwich spread. Cauliflower complements the chicken, making this dish rich in antioxidants as well as vitamins A, B, and E, but it also adds a welcome nutty, roasted flavor and interesting texture. Salty cashews and plump golden raisins balance out the flavors. **Serves 4 to 6**

1 medium head cauliflower, chopped into 2-inch pieces (about 6 cups)

1 tablespoon plus 1 teaspoon canola oil

1 teaspoon hot curry powder

Kosher salt and freshly ground black pepper

1 (1-pound) bone-in, skin-on chicken breast

Mayonnaise

1 egg yolk

1½ teaspoons white wine vinegar

⅛ teaspoon salt

3 grinds black pepper

¼ teaspoon mustard

½ cup canola oil

2 scallions, white and green parts, sliced very thin

½ teaspoon hot curry powder

2 tablespoons grated onion

⅓ cup salted roasted cashews, coarsely chopped

⅓ cup golden raisins

Toasted slices rye, pumpernickel, or other brown bread

TO PREPARE THE CAULIFLOWER AND CHICKEN, arrange 2 racks in the oven and preheat to 400°F. Toss the cauliflower with the 1 tablespoon oil, curry powder, and ¼ teaspoon salt in a bowl, and arrange in a single layer on a rimmed baking sheet or in a glass baking dish. Put the chicken in a roasting pan or on a rimmed baking sheet, brush with the remaining 1 teaspoon oil, and season with salt and pepper. Transfer both to the oven, one on each rack. Roast the cauliflower for 20 minutes. Remove from the oven and let cool. Let the chicken roast for an additional 10 to 15 minutes (30 to 35 minutes total), until a meat thermometer registers 160°F. Remove from the oven and cool.

TO MAKE THE MAYONNAISE, whisk the egg yolk with the vinegar, salt, pepper, and mustard in a bowl. When well combined, begin adding the oil very slowly, a few drops at a time, until about a quarter of the oil has formed a smooth emulsion with the yolk. Add the remaining oil in a slow, steady stream, whisking constantly. To this half-cup of basic mayo, add the scallions, curry powder, and the grated onion. Taste for seasoning and adjust as needed, and refrigerate until ready to use.

TO PREPARE AND SERVE THE SALAD, when the chicken is cool, remove and discard the skin, cut the meat from the bone, and dice it into ½-inch pieces. Give the cauliflower a rough chop so the pieces are no more than ½ inch. In a large bowl, combine the chicken, cauliflower, mayo, cashews, and raisins and toss until well mixed. Taste for seasoning, adding more salt, pepper, or curry if you like. Scoop the salad onto toasted bread and enjoy.

tip: *When making the mayo, pouring the oil from a measuring cup with a spout or squeeze bottle makes it easier to control the flow.*

Tortilla Soup

The recipe variations for Mexico's renowned *sopa de tortilla* are as countless as riffs on Grandma's chicken noodle soup. Its popularity, like Gram's elixir, stems from a soul-satisfying mix of bold and subtle flavors. Our adaptation calls for a traditional pulpy base of pureed roasted vegetables adorned with bits of poached chicken, studs of creamy avocado, and shards of toasty corn tortillas. Its spicy kick comes from a duo of chiles: the fruity poblano and the fiery chipotle. **Serves 4 to 6**

6 cups chicken stock (page 131)

1 bone-in, skinless chicken breast

1/2 cup fresh or frozen corn kernels

1 small yellow onion, cut into large dice (about 1 cup)

1 pound plum tomatoes, peeled, seeded, and roughly chopped.

2 cloves garlic, halved

2 poblano chiles, seeded and cut into large strips

2 teaspoons ground cumin

Kosher salt and freshly ground black pepper

1 tablespoon vegetable oil

3 corn tortillas, brushed with vegetable oil on each side and cut into 1/4-inch strips

1 dried chipotle chile

1 cup loosely packed fresh cilantro leaves, coarsely chopped

1 or 2 sprigs fresh oregano leaves, chopped (1 to 2 teaspoons)

Zest and juice of 1 lime

1 avocado, diced

Sour cream

Preheat the oven to 425°F. Line a rimmed baking sheet with aluminum foil.

TO PREPARE THE CHICKEN, bring the stock to a boil in a large pot over medium heat. Add the chicken, reduce to a simmer, cover, and poach for 15 minutes. Remove the chicken and reserve the stock. When the chicken is cool enough to handle, pull the meat from the bones and set aside.

TO PREPARE THE VEGETABLES AND THE TORTILLA STRIPS, combine the corn, onion, tomatoes, garlic, poblano chiles, cumin, 1 teaspoon salt, 1/4 teaspoon pepper, and the oil in a large bowl, tossing to coat the vegetables with the oil and seasonings. Spread the vegetables on the prepared sheet.

Spread the tortilla strips on a separate baking sheet. Transfer both pans to the oven. Toast the strips for about 10 to 12 minutes, until they are golden brown. Roast the vegetables for 20 minutes, just until they begin to brown at the edges.

While the vegetables are roasting, rehydrate the chipotle chile. Remove its stem, slice it in half, and discard seeds. Soak the pepper in a small bowl of very hot water for 10 minutes.

TO FINISH THE SOUP, return the stock to a simmer and transfer the vegetables from the oven to the pot. Crumble half of the toasted tortilla strips into the stock and add the rehydrated chipotle, discarding the soaking water. Simmer for about 15 minutes.

Add the cilantro and oregano. With a handheld blender, puree the vegetables, tortillas, and herbs into the stock (the chipotle will add significant heat to the soup, so for a milder batch, remove it before blending). If you are using a regular blender, puree the soup in batches and take care to avoid hot splatters. Stir in the chicken and lime zest and juice. Add salt and pepper to taste.

Ladle the soup into bowls and top with the remaining tortilla strips, avocado, and sour cream.

Thai Coconut-Curry Soup

To home cooks, restaurant favorites sometimes feel a bit out of reach. But those fragrant bowls of soup at authentic Thai joints seem much harder to emulate than they actually are. The characteristic mix of sour, sweet, and salty is easy to attain with a combination of supermarket shortcuts (Thai red curry paste) and authentic ingredients—don't even try to skip the lemongrass! Want a vegetarian soup? Just omit the chicken and fish sauce. **Serves 4 to 6**

1 tablespoon vegetable oil

1 clove garlic, minced

1 (1-inch) piece fresh ginger, peeled and minced

$1/2$ teaspoon red curry paste

8 cups chicken stock (page 131) or vegetable broth (page 137)

2 stalks lemongrass, rough tops trimmed and bulbs smashed

1 bone-in, skinless chicken breast (about 6 ounces)

8 ounces rice noodles

2 teaspoons fish sauce

5 fresh basil leaves, thinly sliced

5 fresh mint leaves, thinly sliced

$1/2$ cup coconut milk

2 scallions, white and green parts, thinly sliced

1 lime, half juiced and half cut into wedges

Heat the oil in a medium saucepan over medium-high heat. Add the garlic and ginger and sauté for about 30 seconds, or just until fragrant. Stir in the curry paste. Sauté briefly, then add the stock, mixing to combine. Add the lemongrass and simmer the mixture for about 10 minutes.

Add the chicken and simmer for 15 minutes, or until the internal temperature reads 160°F. Remove the chicken and let cool.

Add the noodles, bring to a boil, and cook until the noodles are just tender.

When the chicken is cool enough to handle, shred it into small pieces and add the meat back into the pot. Stir in the fish sauce, basil, mint, coconut milk, and scallions. Remove the lemongrass and squeeze the lime juice into the soup. Serve the lime wedges with each bowl of soup.

Chicken and Biscuit Pot Pie

Few dishes are more deserving of the comfort food label than chicken and biscuits. And this pie delivers stick-to-your-ribs satisfaction with substantially less meat. Heaps of vegetables nestle in a thick stew that can be made equally delicious with chicken stock or vegetable broth. While home-made versions of both are best, store-bought broths work, too. The whole-grain biscuit topping spreads out like a rustic blanket over the stew. With or without the chicken, this pie is hearty and satisfying. **Serves 6 to 8**

Stew

2 bone-in, skin-on chicken legs, with thighs and drumsticks separated (about 2 pounds total)

Kosher salt and freshly ground black pepper

1 tablespoon olive oil

2 pounds leeks (about 3 very large), white and light green parts only, cut in half lengthwise and then crosswise into $1/2$-inch pieces

$1/4$ cup unbleached all-purpose flour

$1/2$ cup dry white wine

4 cups chicken stock (page 131)

$1/4$ cup whole milk

2 sprigs fresh thyme

2 bay leaves

1 sprig rosemary

4 cloves garlic, halved, peeled, and smashed

1 cup $1/2$-inch carrot chunks (about 2 small carrots)

1 cup diced parsnips (about 2 medium parsnips)

1 cup diced fennel (about $1/2$ small bulb)

4 ounces green beans, sliced into $1/2$-inch pieces (1 cup)

3 tablespoons minced fresh tarragon leaves (optional)

Topping

$1^1/2$ cups whole wheat pastry flour

$1/2$ cup wheat bran

2 teaspoons baking powder

$1/2$ teaspoon baking soda

$1/2$ teaspoon salt

$1/2$ teaspoon freshly ground black pepper

2 tablespoons finely sliced fresh chives or minced scallions

6 tablespoons cold butter, cut into small pieces

1 cup plain low-fat yogurt

TO MAKE THE STEW, rinse the chicken and pat dry with paper towels. Season both sides of the pieces with salt and pepper. Heat the oil in a large Dutch oven over medium-high heat. Add the chicken, skin side down, and cook for about 5 minutes, until nicely browned. Flip the pieces over and brown the other side, for an additional 5 minutes. Transfer the chicken to a plate.

Add the leeks and sauté in the chicken fat for about 7 minutes, until softened. Stir in the flour and cook for 1 minute. Whisk in the wine, scraping up any browned bits. Stir in the stock, milk, thyme, bay leaves, rosemary, and garlic. Return the chicken to the pot, adding any reserved juices. Cover and simmer for about 45 minutes, or until the chicken is fully cooked and just starting to fall off the bone.

continued . . .

Transfer the chicken to a cutting board and remove the skin. Discard the bay leaves, rosemary, and thyme sprigs. Add the carrots, parsnips, fennel, and green beans to the pot. Add the tarragon if you wish. Return the stew to a simmer and season with salt and pepper to taste. When the chicken is cool enough to handle, shred the meat from the bones and add the meat back to the stew. Discard the bones.

TO MAKE THE BISCUIT TOPPING, preheat the oven to 425°F. Whisk together the flour, bran, baking powder, baking soda, salt, pepper, and chives in a bowl. Gently work the cold butter into the dry ingredients, rubbing it together as if you were snapping your fingers. Take care not to overwork the mixture or melt the butter with the warmth of your hands. Once all the butter has been incorporated, add the yogurt and stir just enough to bring the mixture together, forming a damp dough.

Ladle the chicken mixture equally into six heatproof bowls. Drop the biscuit dough by the tablespoonful across the surface of the stew in each bowl. Transfer to the oven and bake for 20 minutes, or until the dough is just golden on top. (Alternatively, leave the chicken mixture in the Dutch oven. Drop the biscuit dough across the surface of the stew, transfer to the oven, and bake for 20 minutes, or until the dough is just golden on top. Serve directly from the pot.)

:tip: *To make this dish vegetarian, simply eliminate the chicken and begin by sautéing the leeks in 2 tablespoons butter. Use vegetable broth to replace the chicken stock, and proceed, simmering all the vegetables for 30 minutes and then adding the biscuit topping as directed.*

WHITE MEAT VS. DARK MEAT

Health nuts are constantly calling for white meat because it's a leaner choice, but dark meat offers moisture and richness. It adds better texture and bigger flavor to a wide variety of dishes. And in reality the nutritional difference is negligible: 3 ounces of dark meat has only 20 extra calories and 2 extra grams of fat. Considering that you also get more vitamins and iron, it's a smart and small splurge, especially when you are cutting back on meat consumption in general. Many of our recipes call for thigh meat: if you haven't cooked with dark meat, you are in for a treat both when you pay for it and when you taste it. It's typically less than half the price of boneless, skinless breasts.

Penne with Chicken Sausage and Broccolini

So many Italian dishes seem effortless. Cooks simply round up pristine ingredients, cook them perfectly, and toss it all together with pasta and cheese. Voilà! They make it look so easy, but what they rarely reveal is their secret ingredient: the starchy pasta cooking water. Added to a flavorful mélange of ingredients, it provides the saucy moisture and thickening power needed to pull a dish together. Here, we use chicken sausage instead of the more traditional pork variety to give the dish some meaty substance while keeping it light and good-for-you. We call for Broccolini, a mild, tender green, though you could substitute the slightly bitter broccoli rabe for more complex flavor.

Serves 4 to 6

$1/4$ cup olive oil, divided

$1/2$ pound Italian chicken sausage

1 pound penne

2 cloves garlic, minced (about 1 tablespoon)

$3/4$ teaspoon dried chile flakes

$1/2$ cup dry white wine

$1^1/2$ cups pasta water

1 bunch (about 1 pound) Broccolini, ends trimmed, then cut into 1-inch pieces

1 teaspoon salt

Freshly grated Parmesan cheese, for serving

Heat 1 tablespoon of the oil over medium-high heat in a large sauté pan until shimmering. Remove the sausage from the casings and crumble into the pan. Cook, stirring occasionally, for 6 to 8 minutes, until brown. Remove from the pan and set aside.

While the sausage is cooking, begin cooking the pasta according to the package directions. Timing is important in this recipe. Be sure all your ingredients are prepped so that the dish comes together quickly. Don't drop the pasta into the boiling water until you are about 10 minutes away from tossing it with the sauce. Add the garlic and chile flakes to the sausage pan, stirring for about 30 seconds, or until fragrant. Pour the wine into the pan and simmer, scraping the browned bits left from the sausage on the bottom, until half of the liquid has evaporated. While the pasta is finishing cooking, ladle $1/2$ cup of the pasta cooking water into the sauté pan, add the Broccolini and salt, cover the pan, and simmer for 2 minutes.

Remove the lid and simmer for another minute, or until the Broccolini is bright green and tender and most of the liquid has evaporated. Ladle an additional $1/2$ cup pasta water into the pan, and then strain the pasta, reserving some of the cooking water. Toss the pasta with the Broccolini and sausage and let the mixture cook for an additional minute so that the pasta begins to soak up some of the flavors and thicken the sauce.

Stir the remaining 3 tablespoons olive oil into the pasta and toss to combine, adding additional pasta water to moisten if desired. Taste for seasoning and adjust as needed. Top individual servings with the Parmesan cheese.

Eggplant and Chicken Puttanesca Stacks

The Italian sauce puttanesca might have a name with naughty implications, but this dish is downright good. Eggplant is a staple ingredient in many cuisines of the world and has been called the poor man's meat. Its hearty texture and smooth mouthfeel lend body and oomph to casseroles, Parmesans (like chicken, veal, and eggplant), stir-fries, sandwiches, and myriad other preparations. In this recipe, crunchy breaded eggplant rounds alternate with thin scaloppine-style chicken medallions bathed in the zesty sauce. Served atop traditionally prepared creamy polenta, supper becomes seduction. **Serves 4 to 6**

Eggplant

2 eggplants (about 1 pound each), cut into $1/2$-inch slices

Kosher salt and freshly ground black pepper

1 cup all-purpose flour, or as needed

2 eggs, beaten

1 cup (2 ounces) panko bread crumbs

3 tablespoons vegetable oil

Chicken

2 boneless, skinless chicken breasts (4 to 6 ounces each)

Kosher salt and freshly ground black pepper

All-purpose flour (use the flour that remains after breading the eggplant)

1 tablespoon olive oil

Sauce and Filling

$1/2$ cup white wine

2 cloves garlic, minced (about 1 tablespoon)

3 anchovy fillets packed in oil, chopped, or $1/2$ teaspoon anchovy paste

$1/4$ teaspoon dried chile flakes

$1/2$ cup chicken stock (page 131)

$1/4$ cup pitted Kalamata olives (about 10 olives or 1.5 ounces), chopped

1 (28-ounce) can diced tomatoes, or 1 pound plum tomatoes, peeled, seeded, and roughly chopped

Zest and juice of $1/2$ lemon

$3/4$ cup loosely packed fresh parsley leaves, coarsely chopped, divided

Kosher salt and freshly ground black pepper

1 cup fresh ricotta cheese, at room temperature

Preheat the oven to 425°F. Line a rimmed baking sheet with aluminum foil.

TO PREPARE THE EGGPLANT, toss with 2 teaspoons salt and let sit in a colander placed over a bowl for about 20 minutes. Pat each piece dry, sprinkle with $1/2$ teaspoon pepper, and proceed with breading.

Put the flour, eggs, and panko in separate shallow bowls or pie plates. First, dip an eggplant slice in the flour, shaking off the excess. Next, coat the floured slice with egg, letting the extra run off. Finally, dredge the eggplant slice in the panko. Repeat with the remaining eggplant. Heat the vegetable oil in a large sauté pan over medium-high heat. Working in batches to avoid overcrowding the pan, fry the eggplant slices for about 2 minutes on each side, or until golden brown. Transfer the eggplant to the prepared baking sheet and bake in the oven for 15 minutes. Flip the slices over and continue baking for an additional 10 minutes.

continued . . .

PREPARE THE CHICKEN WHILE THE EGGPLANT IS IN THE OVEN. Pound each breast to $1/4$-inch thickness with the smooth side of a meat mallet. (If the tender is still attached to the breast, remove it and pound it separately.) Cut each breast into thirds and season the pieces with salt and pepper. Coat each piece in flour and shake off any excess. Wipe the sauté pan clean of remaining breadcrumbs and heat the olive oil in it over medium-high heat. Working in batches, sauté the chicken pieces for about 1 minute on each side, or until lightly browned. Remove the chicken from the pan and cover to keep warm.

TO PREPARE THE SAUCE, pour the wine into the pan to deglaze, scraping the bits from the bottom. Add the garlic, anchovies, and chile flakes and sauté for 30 seconds.

Stir in the stock, olives, tomatoes, lemon juice, and $1/2$ cup of the parsley, and add the chicken back into the pan. Reduce the heat to low and let simmer while the eggplant finishes baking. Taste for seasoning and adjust as needed.

TO PREPARE THE FILLING, mix the cheese, the remaining $1/4$ cup parsley, the lemon zest, 1 teaspoon salt, and $1/4$ teaspoon pepper together in a small bowl. When the eggplant is done, create stacks. Start with one slice of eggplant, top with a dollop of cheese, and then one piece of chicken. Top each stack with a piece of eggplant. If desired, spoon some remaining sauce and cheese on top of each stack and serve.

Chicken Pizza with Arugula Pesto and Sun-Dried Tomatoes

This pizza takes its cue from upscale restaurants where unexpected ingredients take the place of the familiar tomato sauce and mozzarella. We start with a delicious (and wholesome) wheat crust and then top it with a flavorful array of nontraditional pizza ingredients. Sure, we like the tomato sauce and mozzarella, but this version features the kind of bold flavors that can change the way you view pizza night and finally get the pizza shop off your speed dial. We recommend making the dough when you have some extra time and freezing it for a weeknight meal that's quicker and far tastier than delivery. **Makes 2 (12-inch) pizzas**

Dough
2 cups all-purpose flour
2 cups whole wheat flour
2 (7-gram) packets active dry yeast
1½ cups warm water (about 110°F)
1 tablespoon honey
2 teaspoons salt
3 tablespoons olive oil

Pesto
2 cloves garlic
½ cup (2 ounces) grated Parmesan or Romano cheese
½ teaspoon dried chile flakes
1 cup firmly packed coarsely chopped arugula

2 tablespoons pine nuts, toasted
1 tablespoon olive oil

Chicken
2 boneless, skinless chicken thighs (about 6 ounces total)
Salt and freshly ground black pepper
2 teaspoons vegetable oil

Assembly
Cornmeal, about 1 tablespoon for the pizza peel
12 dry-packed sun-dried tomatoes, rehydrated in hot water for 10 minutes
2 cups (about 8 ounces) grated Fontina cheese

Put a pizza stone on your oven's lowest rack and preheat the oven to 500°F.

TO MAKE THE DOUGH, whisk both flours together and set aside. Combine the yeast with ½ cup of the warm water and honey in the bowl of a stand mixer and set aside for 10 minutes. Add the remaining 1 cup water, the salt, olive oil, and about 1 cup of the flour. Whisk by hand, adding more flour until a wet dough (resembling loose oatmeal) forms. Attach the bowl to the mixer, and with the dough hook, mix the dough on low for a minute. Continue mixing, adding the rest of the flour in ½ cup increments. Mix on low speed for 5 minutes to knead the dough. Depending on the humidity of your kitchen, it might seem like you have to add water to the dough, but don't worry—the flour will hydrate over time. Cover, and set aside in a warm place to rise for 1 hour, then punch the dough down and let rise again for another hour. After the second rise, divide in half, forming two dough balls. Set aside on your counter while you prepare the remaining ingredients.

TO MAKE THE PESTO, put the garlic, cheese, and chile flakes in a food processor and pulse until minced. Add the arugula, pine nuts, and olive oil and process until a relatively smooth paste forms.

continued . . .

TO PREPARE THE CHICKEN, pat it dry with a paper towel and season with salt and pepper on each side. Heat the vegetable oil in a sauté pan on medium-high until shimmering but not smoking. Add the chicken and cook for about 2 minutes, until browned. Flip the pieces over and brown the other side, for an additional 2 minutes, and then transfer to a cutting board. When cool enough to handle, cut into 1/4-inch strips and set aside.

TO ASSEMBLE THE PIZZA, roll out the dough to two (12-inch) rounds. Dust a wooden pizza peel with cornmeal, and put a dough round on it to assemble. Top with half the pesto. Scatter half the chicken and sun-dried tomatoes evenly around the pizza. Top with half the cheese. Using the peel, shimmy your pizza directly onto your preheated pizza stone. Assemble second pie while the first one is in the oven. Bake for 10 to 12 minutes, until the cheese is brown and bubbly.

> **tip** *If you don't have a stand mixer, you can make the dough by hand. Incorporate the flour 1/2 cup at a time by stirring with a spoon until you can lift the dough out of the bowl as a soft ball. Transfer to a floured surface and continue to add the remaining flour, kneading it in a little at a time. Once all of the flour has been added, continue to knead the dough for about 10 minutes, or until it is soft and smooth. Add the flour to the kneading surface sparingly so as to avoid drying out the dough.*

SAFETY FIRST

The Centers for Disease Control report about 40,000 cases of illness caused by salmonella every year. When it comes to chicken, a common carrier of bacteria, cooks are justifiably concerned about safe handling. When you bring your poultry home from the market, your first step should be to keep it cold. Stash it on a dish or tray (to trap any runaway juices) in the lowest part of your refrigerator. Opinions about safe internal temperatures for the finished bird range from the ultra conservative 185°F to the riskier 140°F. The U.S. Food Safety & Inspections Service recommends cooking to 165°F to be sure salmonella is eliminated. Our recipes suggest you cook chicken until it reaches 160°F; for us it's plenty safe and allows the meat to retain some moisture. Proper refrigeration and cooking are fundamental to food safety, but they won't protect you from lackadaisical cleaning habits. It's best to designate separate cutting boards for meats and vegetables. And always wash boards and tools in hot soapy water after use.

A Taste of Turkey

Turkey's potential goes far beyond holiday dinner tables to last the entire year.

Thanksgiving dinner is the one time each year when all eyes are on turkey. Ben Franklin, who wanted to make the North American wild turkey our national bird, would be so disappointed that the rest of the time, turkey is relegated to sandwiches wolfed down at our desks or flavorless turkey burgers ordered to save the fat and calories of a beef burger, not for the love of the bird. Few would list turkey as a favorite food, and it's rarely featured on restaurant menus. But just like chicken, it can be versatile and satisfying.

Another thing turkey has in common with chicken is that the vast majority of what's available comes from factory farms, where the Broadbreasted White is the only breed raised. This now ubiquitous bird resulted from generations of selective breeding. Farmers were on a quest to create a bird with the maximum amount of white meat. They have been freakishly successful; the Broadbreasted White is so top heavy that it can't walk, fly, or even reproduce on its own. Without human assistance, this avian science experiment would die out in a single generation.

But its unnatural physique isn't the only problem with this bird's dominance in the market. Like most products of factory farming, conventionally produced turkeys eat a scientifically formulated feed that includes antibiotics to keep them alive until large enough to slaughter. If these ethical issues don't change your shopping habits, tasting the alternative might persuade you. There's a growing interest in heritage breeds like the Standard Bronze, Bourbon Red, Narragansett, and Jersey Buff. For many, it's this distinctive taste—something that came close to being lost—that makes heritage turkeys a culinary winner. In recent years, farmers across the United States have seen demand outpace supply for these better-tasting birds for Thanksgiving feasts.

Around the holidays, people think more about the food they will cook and eat. But what about all those sandwiches, burgers, and slices of turkey bacon we eat the rest of the time? We suggest forgoing lunchmeat—which is typically processed with additives and preservatives—because its flavor and texture can't compare to the turkey you roast and slice at home. If you live in a household of one or two, find a specialty market that roasts organic turkeys and buy your sliced turkey there. You will be rewarded with tastier sandwiches and a clear conscience.

Factory farming's full complement of consequences has yet to emerge. Scientists are now investigating the effect that additives in animal feed have on the soil and water. Each year, when supermarkets run promotions that reward shoppers with a "free turkey" for spending a certain amount of money, the prize is a factory-farmed Broadbreasted White. Before you claim that free turkey, consider the hidden costs to your health and the environment.

GIVING THANKS FOR **TURKEY PARTS**

The key to putting turkey to good culinary use beyond the Thanksgiving table is learning how to cook with more manageable turkey parts. Unless you have a family of twelve, it just doesn't make sense to roast a 20-pound bird except for a holiday feast. Supermarkets often have a decent selection of cuts, but it's helpful to get a guided tour from a real butcher. These experts can assist you with finding your favorite cut—and just the right amount—of this inexpensive meat. In the meantime, here's a primer to get you started.

Breast: Turkey breasts are all white meat, low in cholesterol, fat, and sodium. They can range in size from 3 to 9 pounds and are available whole or split, with or without the bone and skin. They can be roasted, sliced, and served hot or cold. Turkey chops are cross cuts of bone-in turkey breasts, usually cut about 1 inch thick. A small turkey breast can serve 4 people as a main course, or up to 8 in recipes like ours.

London broil: This cut is a boneless, skinless breast half that has been butterflied (cut almost completely in half and opened like a book). It's an excellent cut to marinate or grill. It ranges in size from $1^1/_2$ to $4^1/_2$ pounds and will serve at least 4 and up to 8 or 10 if used in a recipe like Chimichurri Fajitas in the place of beef (page 94).

Tenderloin: Similar to a chicken tender, this cut is the small piece of white meat on the underside of the breast.

It is boneless and skinless, usually weighs between 6 and 12 ounces, and will serve 2 to 4 depending on how it's used. The tenderloin is a good cut for recipes calling for smaller quantities of meat like Turkey Verde Soup (page 40). Tenderloins can also be sliced and pounded thin.

Cutlets: Thin slices of white meat breast or tenderloin, turkey cutlets usually weigh about 4 ounces depending on thickness. Cutlets are perfect for recipes calling for a smaller quantity of turkey breast and can also be cooked in the same manner as chicken or veal cutlets.

Legs and thighs: The dark meat of the turkey is available bone-in or boneless, with or without skin. Legs, or drumsticks, are usually sold bone-in with skin. Both cuts are excellent for all methods of cooking and take very well to marinades and brines. Bone-in legs and thighs can weigh in at around

---

2 pounds each and will yield several servings in a recipe like African Peanut Stew (page 35).

Ground: You can find ground turkey available in packages containing all white meat, all dark, or a mix of both. Ground dark meat is sometimes called turkey burger and is usually moister and more flavorful than ground white meat, which tends to dry out easily. Ground turkey can be substituted for ground beef in most recipes and is sold by the pound. A half-pound of ground turkey yields 4 servings in our recipe for Tofu-Turkey Sloppy Joes (page 38).

Wings: All white meat available whole or as wing tips, wings are excellent for adding flavor and depth to soups and stocks.

Neck: The collagen richness of the neck makes it an MVP for stocks.

Giblets: The liver, heart, and gizzard are sometimes simmered with vegetables in water to make a flavorful liquid for the base of gravies.

African Peanut Stew

In Africa, home cooking means hearty stews served over rice or mashed root vegetables. Peanuts, known as groundnuts there, lend flavor and texture to our version of a traditional West African recipe. Okra, another staple in African cuisine, does what it does best, thickening the liquid as it simmers in the broth with tomatoes and vitamin- and iron-rich Swiss chard. Creating a vegetarian version of this stew is simple: switch to vegetable broth and omit the turkey, adding chunks of tofu or cooked beans (such as kidney) for meaty texture. **Serves 4 to 6**

2 tablespoons vegetable oil, divided

1 (12-ounce) boneless, skinless turkey thigh, cut into 1-inch strips

1/4 cup water

4 ounces okra (about 12), sliced into 1/4-inch rounds

1 medium yellow onion, sliced into 1/8-inch strips

4 cups roasted turkey stock (page 132)

2 cloves garlic, chopped

1/4 teaspoon cayenne pepper

2 teaspoons garam masala

1 cup canned or fresh diced tomatoes

1/2 cup smooth natural peanut butter

4 cups 1/4-inch ribbons sliced Swiss or red chard (about 15 leaves)

4 to 6 cups cooked white rice

1 small red bell pepper, cut into 1/4-inch dice (about 1 cup)

1/4 cup roasted salted peanuts, coarsely chopped

6 scallions, white and green parts, thinly sliced

Heat 1 tablespoon of the vegetable oil in a large Dutch oven over medium-high heat. Add the turkey and cook for about 5 minutes, just until the meat is lightly browned. Transfer the meat and juices to a plate. Add the water and deglaze the pot, scraping up the bits from the bottom. Pour the liquid and bits over the reserved turkey.

Reduce the heat to medium and add the remaining tablespoon oil to the pot. Add the okra and sauté for about 5 minutes, until a shiny, sticky film forms. Add the onion and cook for an additional 5 minutes. Pour in 1/2 cup of the stock and deglaze the bottom of the pot.

Add the garlic and cook for about 30 seconds, just until fragrant. Stir in the cayenne, garam masala, tomatoes, peanut butter, reserved turkey and juices, remaining stock, and chard. Simmer over medium-low heat for 45 minutes. Taste for seasoning and adjust as needed.

Serve the stew over hot cooked rice and sprinkle with red pepper, peanuts, and scallions.

> :tip: *Garam masala is a North Indian blend of spices, which usually includes cinnamon, cloves, cumin, cardamom, nutmeg, black pepper, and chiles. It can be found at specialty shops and some supermarkets. It's true that most commercially sold curry powders are also a blend of spices, but garam masala's constituents make for a different flavor profile. So while this recipe would still be delicious using curry powder as a substitute for garam masala, it wouldn't be quite the same.*

Turkey BLT with Chipotle Avocado

Typically, we cry foul at a BLT without mayo. For us, the creamy spread is essential on this classic sandwich. But, in the case of our TBLT, we replace the condiment with a velvety smooth avocado puree spiked with smoky hot chipotles. As is the case with its porky brethren, the turkey bacon, lettuce, and tomato sandwich is highly customizable. Use thick-cut turkey bacon for some chew or thinner slices if you want crunch. Whichever you choose, we're sure you'll love this version . . . even if we catch you sneaking on a schmear of mayonnaise. **Serves 4**

8 strips (about 8 ounces) turkey bacon

1 avocado, diced (about 1 cup)

Kosher salt and freshly ground black pepper

$1/4$ teaspoon white wine vinegar or lime juice

1 chipotle in adobo sauce

8 slices white bread, toasted

4 large lettuce leaves (romaine, Boston, Bibb, or green or red leaf)

1 pound tomatoes, sliced to desired thickness

Preheat the oven to 400°F.

Line a rimmed baking sheet with aluminum foil, parchment paper, or a silicone mat. Place the bacon strips on the sheet, about 1 inch apart. Transfer to the oven and bake for 10 to 15 minutes, to desired doneness.

While the bacon cooks, put the avocado, $1/4$ teaspoon salt, and the vinegar in a blender or food processor. Cut off the stem of the chipotle, halve it lengthwise, and scrape out the seeds. Coarsely chop the chipotle and add it to the blender. (Use just half of the chipotle if you prefer less heat.) Blend the ingredients to a smooth, spreadable consistency. Cover the surface of the avocado spread with plastic wrap until ready to use.

When the bacon is ready, assemble the sandwich. Spread about 1 tablespoon of the avocado chipotle mixture on one slice of the toasted bread. Add the lettuce, tomato, and two slices of bacon. Season with salt and pepper, and top with the other slice of toasted bread.

:tip: *Cooking turkey bacon is as much a matter of taste as the construction of the BLT. Baking (as directed in this recipe), pan frying, broiling, and microwaving all produce different results—just master the process to your liking. Turkey bacon is very low in fat, so when pan frying, add a bit of butter or oil to a skillet over medium-high heat, then add the bacon strips and cook to desired doneness. (Don't crowd the pan or the pieces will steam instead of frying up crisp.) Broiling can be effective but tricky; if you don't watch it closely, you can start a fire. If you opt for the microwave, lay bacon strips about $1/2$ inch apart on a microwave-safe plate, cover with a paper towel, and cook on regular power, for 1 minute per slice.*

BRING HOME **THE BACON**

Turkey bacon has long been considered a health-conscious substitute for traditional pork bacon. We'd never suggest you completely eliminate pork bacon from your diet, but in many recipes, especially on sandwiches, with your breakfast, or as a salad topper, turkey bacon is just as satisfying with much less fat and fewer calories.

The first commandment of all smart supermarket shopping: thou shalt read ingredients labels carefully. This list is even more important than the nutrition information, especially when it comes to turkey bacon. Most consumers are completely unaware that many brands start with mechanically separated turkey—a paste-like byproduct created by putting turkey bones through a high-pressure system that strips the bones of every last molecule of meat. As you can imagine, this "meat" actually contains calcium since it includes trace amounts of bone. Because of concerns about mad cow disease, the process is illegal in beef processing. Chicken, turkey, and pork are all fair game. A turkey bacon that lists turkey thighs—not mechanically separated turkey—as its first ingredient is more wholesome and will almost certainly taste better.

You may also want to avoid ingredients like sodium nitrite, a controversial preservative that recent studies have linked to cancer, and autolyzed yeast extract, a common additive that is essentially just another phrase for MSG. A good turkey bacon's list of ingredients will be short and easy to understand. Our favorite brand contains only turkey, salt, sugar, beet powder, paprika, onion powder, and water. Another good option is buying your turkey bacon from a reputable, old-fashioned butcher.

Tofu-Turkey Sloppy Joes

Few foods have the power of childhood favorites. Hot dogs, mac and cheese, and sloppy joes all recall a time when we didn't worry about cholesterol. This part-tofu take on a classic sandwich offers a taste of nostalgia without the guilt. (If tofu really doesn't appeal to you, it's just as good made with a pound of ground turkey, but we encourage you to try it. Tofu-hating testers of the recipe were surprised by the great taste.) And if you want to make a vegetarian version, simply use all tofu instead (see page 57 for preparation instructions), though you will also need to omit the Worcestershire—its savory kick comes from anchovies. Hops and malt give beer its flavor and lend depth to this recipe, but you may omit it and use the same amount of water instead. **Serves 4**

2 tablespoons canola oil, divided

1 small onion, cut into ¼-inch dice (about 1 cup)

1 small red bell pepper, cut into ¼-inch dice (about ½ cup)

1 stalk celery, cut into ¼-inch dice (about ¼ cup)

3 cloves garlic, minced

8 ounces ground turkey

8 ounces extra-firm tofu, pressed (see page 57) and crumbled to resemble ground meat

1 (8-ounce) can tomato sauce

1 tablespoon molasses

2 tablespoons Worcestershire sauce

1 teaspoon Dijon mustard

1 teaspoon ground cumin

½ cup beer

¼ cup water

1 tablespoon malt vinegar

Salt and pepper

4 soft white hamburger rolls

Butter, for toasted buns (optional)

Grated cheddar cheese, for topping (optional)

Minced onions or scallions, for topping (optional)

Heat 1 tablespoon of the oil in a large skillet over medium-high heat. Add the onion and sauté for about 3 minutes, until translucent and beginning to soften. Add the bell pepper and celery and sauté for an additional 2 to 3 minutes. Stir in the garlic and sauté for about 30 seconds, just until fragrant. Transfer the mixture to a bowl and set aside.

Add the remaining 1 tablespoon oil to the same skillet and return it to the heat. Drop the turkey into the hot pan in small chunks and brown for about 5 minutes, stirring and chopping occasionally. Add the tofu and sauté for 2 minutes more.

While the meat and tofu brown, in a bowl whisk together the tomato sauce, molasses, Worcestershire, mustard, and cumin.

Push the meat and tofu off to one side of the pan and deglaze the bottom by adding the beer, a little at a time, scraping as it bubbles and steams. Stir in the rest of the beer, the onion mixture, tomato sauce mixture, water, and vinegar. Cover the pan, reduce the heat to medium, and simmer for about 15 minutes, stirring once or twice. Taste for seasoning and adjust as needed.

Toast and lightly butter the buns. Add about a cup of filling, topping with grated cheddar and minced onions if you like.

Turkey Verde Soup

Plantains are the chameleon cousin of bananas. Unripe, they can be used as a starchy vegetable; fully ripened, the sweet, creamy flesh is perfect in desserts. In this rendition of white chili, green plantains lend body to the stock, which becomes the backdrop for tart, tangy tomatillos, fiery specks of jalapeño, and satisfying mouthfuls of turkey cubes and soft white beans. Emerald gems of bell peppers add a sweet crunch to the soup sprinkled on top just before slurping. **Serves 4 to 6**

1 tablespoon vegetable oil

8 ounces turkey breast, cutlet, or London broil, cut into $1/2$-inch cubes

1 large green plantain, cut into $1/4$-inch dice (about 1 cup)

1 small yellow onion, cut into $1/4$-inch dice (about 1 cup)

2 cloves garlic, minced (about 1 tablespoon)

1 small jalapeño, stem and seeds removed, cut into $1/8$-inch dice (about 1 tablespoon)

5 cups roasted turkey stock (page 132)

4 medium tomatillos, cut into $1/4$-inch dice (about $11/2$ cups)

$11/2$ cups cooked white beans, such as Great Northern or cannellini, or 1 (15-ounce) can, drained and rinsed

2 teaspoons chopped fresh oregano leaves (about 2 sprigs)

2 teaspoons kosher salt

$1/2$ teaspoon freshly ground black pepper

1 green bell pepper, cut into small dice (optional)

Heat the oil in a Dutch oven or pot over medium-high heat. Brown the turkey quickly, for about 2 minutes, remove from the pot, and set aside.

Add the plantain and onion to the pot and sauté for 3 minutes. Add the garlic and jalapeño and cook for about 30 seconds. Pour in $1/2$ cup of the stock to deglaze the pot, scraping the bits from the bottom. Add the tomatillos, beans, turkey, and the remaining $41/2$ cups stock. Simmer the soup, partially covered, for about 30 minutes, or until the ingredients are tender and the flavors have blended.

Stir in the oregano, salt, and pepper, and simmer for an additional 5 minutes. Taste for seasoning and adjust as needed. Ladle the soup into bowls and top with bell peppers if you wish.

Turkey and Pinto Bean Corn Bread Pie

Without kneading or waiting, the crust of this pie poofs impressively with the boost from yeast and the slow rise of hot air in an oven that hasn't been preheated. The signature tang of the yeast combines with a crunchy corn texture to create a base for meaty ground turkey and pinto beans seasoned with a homemade blend of spices. **Serves 4 to 6**

Salsa

1 cup fresh or canned diced tomatoes

$1/2$ cup loosely packed fresh cilantro leaves, chopped

1 clove garlic, minced to a paste with $1/2$ teaspoon kosher salt

1 tablespoon minced shallot

1 tablespoon seeded and diced jalapeño

$1/2$ teaspoon white wine vinegar

Kosher salt and freshly ground black pepper

Filling

2 teaspoons vegetable oil

8 ounces ground turkey thigh

2 cloves garlic, chopped

1 cup cooked pinto beans, or about $1/3$ (15-ounce) can, drained and rinsed

1 tablespoon ancho chile powder

2 teaspoons ground cumin

Kosher salt and freshly ground black pepper

$1/2$ cup water

Corn Bread Crust

$3/4$ cup cornmeal

$1/2$ cup all-purpose flour

1 teaspoon salt

1 cup corn kernels (fresh, frozen, or canned)

1 tablespoon seeded and diced jalapeño

1 egg, lightly beaten

2 tablespoons vegetable oil

2 tablespoons honey

$3/4$ cup warm whole milk (about 120°F)

2 (7-gram) packets active dry yeast

$1/2$ cup grated cheddar or jack cheese

Sour cream for garnish

Brush a 9-inch pie dish lightly with oil or butter.

TO MAKE THE SALSA, mix together the tomatoes, cilantro, garlic, shallot, jalapeño, and vinegar in a bowl. Set aside to let the flavors come together. Taste for seasoning and adjust as needed.

TO MAKE THE FILLING, heat the oil in a large skillet over medium-high heat. Brown the turkey, stirring occasionally, for about 8 minutes. Add the garlic, beans, chile powder, cumin, and 1 teaspoon salt. Mix the ingredients together and sauté briefly until the garlic and spices are fragrant. Add the water, reduce the heat to medium, and simmer until most of the liquid is gone, scraping the bottom of the pan occasionally. Season to taste with salt and pepper. Remove from the heat.

TO MAKE THE CRUST, in a bowl, mix together the cornmeal, flour, salt, corn, jalapeño, egg, oil, honey, milk, and yeast. Pour the batter into the pie dish. Top with the meat, beans, salsa and cheese.

Set the dish atop a rimmed baking sheet in a cold oven. Set the oven to 375°F and bake for 30 to 40 minutes, until the corn bread crust is golden brown. Remove from the oven and let the pie sit for about 10 minutes before cutting into wedges and serving with dollops of sour cream.

Smoked Turkey Nachos

If you invite friends over for the Super Bowl, be warned: football equals nachos. But this iconic party food doesn't require a greasy mound of ground beef or neon yellow cheesefood. Our version calls on the usual ingredient list plus a few nontraditional items like caramelized onions and smoked turkey legs to provide satisfying layers of flavor. Friends will love digging into this high-piled platter in front of the game. Just make sure you have that other Super Bowl Sunday staple—beer—to wash it down and toast your team's big win. **Serves 6**

2 tablespoons olive oil

1$^{1}/_{2}$ cups thinly sliced white or yellow onion (about 1 medium onion)

2 tablespoons balsamic vinegar

$^{1}/_{4}$ pound smoked turkey leg meat, shredded

$^{1}/_{3}$ cup tomato puree

$^{1}/_{4}$ cup water

1 teaspoon chili powder

2 teaspoons ground cumin

Pinch of cayenne pepper

$^{1}/_{2}$ teaspoon unsweetened cocoa powder

1 (12-ounce) bag tortilla chips

1$^{1}/_{2}$ cups dried black beans, cooked, or 1 (15-ounce) can, drained and rinsed

1 jalapeño, seeded and sliced into thin disks

8 ounces cheddar cheese

4 scallions, white and green parts, sliced

Sour cream for garnish

Preheat the oven to 375°F.

Heat the oil in a large skillet over medium heat. Add the onion and vinegar, and then reduce the heat to medium low. Cook the onion for about 15 minutes, until soft. Add the turkey, tomato puree, water, chili powder, cumin, cayenne, and cocoa powder. Cook for an additional 10 minutes. Taste for seasoning and adjust as needed.

Create one layer of chips in a baking dish. Layer with half of the onion and turkey mixture, beans, jalapeño, and cheese. Repeat with another layer of chips and the remaining ingredients. Transfer the dish to the oven and bake for about 5 minutes, just until the cheese melts. Top with scallions and sour cream.

> tip: *The smoked turkey adds an excellent dimension to these nachos, but they can be made meat free if you choose. Eliminate the shredded turkey and continue with the recipe as is, or replace it with pinto beans for a meaty substitute. Try adding chipotle chile powder or smoked paprika if you want a smoky flavor.*

Vegetable Ragu Lasagne

Often prepared with heaps of beef-based sauce, lasagne is a comfort food casserole that can easily become greasy and heavy. This version isn't low fat or low cal, but it is packed with five kinds of nutrient-rich vegetables and only 6 ounces of meat. The secret is the long slow simmer of the vegetables, which makes a sweet and savory base for the hearty sauce. The ground turkey can simply be omitted for a vegetarian dish. And for those looking to cut fat and calories, it's as easy as using part-skim cheeses. This casserole can feed a crowd or be portioned and frozen for a microwavable office lunch or dinner for one. **Serves 8**

3 tablespoons olive oil

1 large onion, cut into $1/4$-inch dice (1$1/4$ cups)

2 carrots, cut into $1/4$-inch dice (1 cup)

2 stalks celery, cut into $1/4$-inch dice ($1/2$ cup)

Kosher salt and freshly ground black pepper

6 ounces ground turkey thigh

1 (28-ounce) can whole plum tomatoes

3 cups ricotta cheese

1 egg

1 (10-ounce) package frozen spinach, defrosted and squeezed dry

2 cloves garlic, minced

$3/4$ cup freshly grated Parmesan cheese (3 ounces)

1 (9-ounce) box no-boil lasagne noodles (12 noodles)

1$1/4$ cups grated mozzarella

Preheat the oven to 325°F.

TO PREPARE THE SAUCE, heat 2 tablespoons of the oil over medium heat in a heavy Dutch oven. Add the onion, carrots, celery, and $1/4$ teaspoon salt to the pan, and cook, stirring occasionally, for at least 40 minutes and up to 1 hour, until the vegetables are very soft and turning brown. (If your vegetables seem to be browning too quickly, turn the heat down.) Transfer the vegetables to a plate and set aside. Add the ground turkey to the pan and let sit for two minutes to brown before stirring and breaking up the meat, for 2 to 3 more minutes, until cooked through. Return the vegetables to the pan and combine with the turkey. Add the tomatoes, crushed by hand or pulsed with a stick blender, and simmer for 10 minutes.

TO PREPARE THE RICOTTA MIXTURE, while the vegetables are cooking, combine the ricotta cheese, egg, spinach, garlic, Parmesan cheese, $1/4$ teaspoon salt, and $1/8$ teaspoon pepper in a bowl. Set aside.

TO ASSEMBLE THE LASAGNE, brush a 9 by 13-inch pan with oil. Start building the lasagne with a layer of about 1 cup sauce, followed by three noodles, spaced an inch apart. Layer about a quarter of the ricotta mixture on the noodles, followed by $1/4$ cup of mozzarella. Build three more layers, with a final layer of noodles, sauce, and a generous $1/2$ cup mozzarella on top. Cover tightly with aluminum foil and bake for 40 minutes. Uncover and bake for another 20 minutes, broiling for the last few minutes if you like a browned crust. Let the lasagne sit for 20 minutes before serving.

A Little
Fish and Seafood

*Knowing the origin of the fish you buy will help you
make delicious, wholesome meals without any catches.*

Fish has a reputation as a Goody Two-shoes food. Loved by dieters, lauded by doctors, seafood always has a place of honor at the table. Fish and shellfish cook fast and pair beautifully with a large assortment of sauces and condiments. Who in their right mind would go without this light, nutritious food that lends itself to sandwiches and soups as well more elegant preparations? Well, lately, as studies show that many fish contain high levels of mercury and the effects of overfishing become more and more obvious, some thoughtful consumers are scaling back on seafood. And while fish remains an important source of the health-boosting omega-3 fatty acids, it's key to educate yourself about the best choices for your health and the ocean's.

Overfishing simply means that so many fish of a particular species are being caught that the population is threatened. Because the ocean is full of complex and interconnected ecosystems, this has a ripple effect on the planet's overall well-being. By some estimates, 90 percent of the fish we eat are being fished at or over the capacity of what is sustainable. It will take global political action and better regulation to avert a crisis; one step you can take is to be aware of politicians' views on the matter before casting your ballot in local and national elections. Something else you can do is become aware of the most threatened species and avoid buying them. Download a wallet guide to seafood at blueocean.org to refer to in the market and at restaurants.

Unfortunately, overfishing isn't the only threat to our oceans. Many types of farm-raised fish pose hazards as well. Aquaculture, as fish farming is also known, provides a full third of all seafood in the world. Salmon is a good example of the problems with some farmed fish. Like factory farms on land, salmon farms pack a lot of fish into a confined space. Instead of what they would typically eat in the wild, a natural diet that gives them their striking pink hue and their characteristic flavor, farmed salmon eat feed, typically pellets that contain a chemical to turn them pink. The result is flavorless fillets lower in omega-3 fatty acids. The feed typically contains antibiotics to keep farmed fish alive in these less-than-natural living conditions. Finally, when these farmed fish escape into the ocean they interbreed with wild salmon and the offspring do not fare well in the wild.

And if you've ever sampled wild salmon, you know its robust flavor has little in common with the more common farmed variety. But not all aquaculture is created equal. Many species, including some tilapia, clams, mussels, and oysters, can be farmed sustainably. As with overfishing, education is your key to being a responsible consumer.

Mercury is another major concern for those who enjoy seafood. It's found in trace amounts in all fish because it occurs naturally in the environment. But it can be toxic, especially for unborn babies and young children, when it exceeds safe levels in bigger fish that live longer, including tuna, swordfish, shark, king mackerel, and tilefish. For most people, it's not a huge concern. The human body easily rids itself of small amounts of mercury. The occasional large fish isn't going to pose a threat to your health. But remember, if you are pregnant or hoping to become pregnant, you should avoid these types of fish.

The news can be scary, but learning how to shop responsibly will allow you to navigate the waters of cooking with seafood. And, as with all our recipes, a less-is-more approach to these ingredients will save you both money and worries. It is still true that fish is packed with nutrients and is generally lower in fat and calories than other animal proteins. And, of course, few things are as delicious as fresh, high-quality seafood.

BEFRIEND YOUR **FISHMONGER**

The idea of the supermarket is so appealing. Everything you need in one place—bread, milk, eggs, meats, fish, cheese, and laundry detergent, too. But few shoppers stop to consider what we've given up for all this convenience. Once upon a time, people got their groceries from real experts: artisan bakers, skilled butchers, and seasoned fishmongers who knew the provenance of everything in the display case. These purveyors had all but disappeared from our shopping landscape until renewed public interest in recent years has revived some of these old-fashioned trades. If you have a fish market in your neighborhood, make friends with the people who work there. Usually they can provide a mountain of information about your local fish as well as what's been imported. Not only can a fishmonger buddy offer you cooking tips and an informed opinion on what is really the best catch of the day, they can hook you up with free fish trimmings—perfect for making stock (page 134). Fishmongers will often do the work of cleaning and dressing your fish for you, a service you're unlikely to encounter at big grocery chains.

Whitefish and Herbed Cream Cheese Sandwich

A New York–style deli piles enough smoked whitefish salad on its overstuffed sandwiches to last most people a week. Our whitefish sandwich calls for much less fish but doesn't skimp on flavor. Quickly pickled cucumbers lend a bright crunch, and a creamy dill and chive spread pairs perfectly with the smoky fish. We follow the deli's lead with toasted rye bread, lettuce, and tomato. All you need is a side of slaw and a jumbo black and white cookie to round out the meal. **Serves 4**

1/2 teaspoon sugar

1/4 teaspoon salt

2 tablespoons white wine vinegar

1 small cucumber, cut into 1/8-inch slices

1/4 cup loosely packed fresh dill fronds, chopped

2 tablespoons chopped fresh chives

4 ounces cream cheese, at room temperature

8 pieces thinly sliced rye bread, toasted

4 ounces smoked whitefish, crumbled

1 tomato, sliced

2 cups mixed greens

In a bowl, whisk the sugar and salt into the vinegar to dissolve. Pour over the cucumber slices in a zippered storage bag or large bowl and let soak in the refrigerator for at least 30 minutes. Fold the dill and chives into the cream cheese. (A handheld electric mixer helps to soften the cheese and distribute the herbs.)

Spread a thin layer of herbed cream cheese across each piece of toast and evenly distribute the whitefish. Top with pickled cucumbers, tomato, mixed greens, and another slice of toast.

Tuna Tartine

We Americans have our signature sandwiches: heroes, hoagies, grinders, subs. The French have theirs, too: the *tartine* is an open-faced sandwich on toasted, buttered bread, topped with a variety of ingredients. While slimmer than our bulky bunch, *tartines* are packed with as much satisfying flavor. This sandwich takes its cue from the classic salade niçoise, where tuna, beans, hard-boiled eggs, tomatoes, olives, and herbs mingle for a crisp meal popular in the French Riviera city for which it's named. Our version might make every other tuna sandwich seem so passé.

Serves 4 to 6

1 (12-ounce) can tuna packed in water, drained

2 tablespoons pine nuts, toasted

1 hard-boiled egg, cooled and chopped

1/4 cup pitted niçoise or picholine olives, chopped

1 tomato, diced (about 1 cup)

1/2 cup dried white beans, cooked, or about 1/3 (15-ounce) can, drained and rinsed

1 stalk celery, chopped into 1/4-inch-thick pieces

2 tablespoons minced red onion

1/4 cup loosely packed fresh parsley leaves, coarsely chopped

1/4 teaspoon Dijon mustard

Pinch of sugar

2 tablespoons freshly squeezed lemon juice

3 tablespoons olive oil

Butter for toast (optional)

Crusty French bread (boule or baguette), sliced 1/2 inch thick, toasted

In a bowl, combine the tuna, pine nuts, egg, olives, tomato, beans, celery, onion, and parsley. In a small bowl, whisk together the mustard, sugar, and lemon juice. Slowly whisk in the oil until a smooth emulsion forms. Pour the vinaigrette over the tuna mixture and toss gently to coat.

Butter each piece of toast if you wish and top with a few heaping spoonfuls of tuna salad.

Smoked Trout Chowder

In matters of chowder, New England's cream-based clam version is the icon. But a region that has its own argot—"chowda"—for that classic soup is bound to turn out more than one version. This recipe for an old-fashioned fish chowder calls on smoked trout to lend even more depth to an already flavorful pot. The liquid is loaded with texture from chunks of fish and vegetables, but it's not thick from heavy doses of cream. Whole milk adds body and carries the smoky notes without making this chowder too rich. **Serves 4 to 6**

1 tablespoon butter

2 medium leeks, white and light green parts only, cut lengthwise and thinly sliced (about 1 1/2 cups)

2 stalks celery, cut into 1/2-inch dice (about 1 1/2 cups)

1 medium carrot, cut into 1/2-inch dice (about 1 1/2 cups)

2 cloves garlic, minced (about 1 tablespoon)

2 medium Yukon gold potatoes, cut into 1-inch chunks

2 cups water

1/2 pound hot- or cold-smoked trout, broken into chunks

3 cups whole milk

Kosher salt and freshly ground black pepper

2 tablespoons chopped fresh chives

Chowder crackers

Melt the butter in a Dutch oven over medium-high heat. Add the leeks and cook for about 7 minutes, until they begin to soften. Add the celery and carrot and cook for 5 minutes more. Add the garlic and sauté for about 30 seconds. Add the potatoes and water, bring the liquid to a simmer, and cook for 10 minutes. Add the trout to the pot along with the milk. Reduce the heat to medium and simmer for 30 minutes (do not boil).

Season to taste with salt and pepper. Ladle into bowls, sprinkle with chopped chives, and serve with chowder crackers.

Roasted Salmon Citrus Salad

Salmon lends itself to a variety of cooking methods. Its versatility combined with its healthy doses of heart-helpful omega-3 fatty acids makes salmon an excellent addition to the menu. For all the good it does for us, though, we consumers should take care in selecting our sources for the sake of sustaining the species. Wild salmon is preferred to farmed not just for flavor, texture, and natural color but also because salmon farming has proved to have a negative impact on the environment (see page 45). Today, wild Atlantic salmon is nearly extinct, making the Pacific Ocean the most viable source. Look for wild salmon during its peak season, from the spring through the fall. If you have trouble locating wild salmon, substitute any firm-fleshed fish in this recipe. **Serves 4 to 6**

1 teaspoon ground coriander

1 teaspoon smoked paprika

$1/4$ teaspoon kosher salt

12 ounces center-cut wild salmon, cut into 2- or 3-ounce pieces

1 ripe mango, cut into $1/4$-inch dice (about $1/2$ cup)

Zest of $1/2$ lime

$1/4$ cup freshly squeezed lime juice (about 4 limes)

2 tablespoons olive oil

1 head frisée, torn into pieces

1 medium daikon radish, cut into $1/8$-inch strips

1 medium fennel bulb, cut into $1/8$-inch strips

1 cup loosely packed fennel fronds

$1/2$ small red onion, sliced very thin

1 orange, cut into segments

Preheat the oven to 400°F. Lightly oil a baking dish.

In a small bowl, mix the coriander, paprika, and salt together and rub evenly on each piece of fish. Transfer the fish to the prepared baking dish and roast for 15 minutes. Remove from the oven and let cool slightly.

Make the dressing by pureeing the mango, lime zest, lime juice, and oil in a blender until smooth. In a bowl, toss the frisée, daikon radish, fennel bulb, fennel fronds, onion, and orange segments with the dressing. Top with the salmon and serve.

Shrimp and Slow-Roasted Tomato Risotto

Risotto is so misunderstood. Thought to be a luxurious restaurant dish, risotto is actually much better at home, where you can make it to order. (At a restaurant, the rice is often cooked hours ahead.) Because of its creamy texture, dieters typically avoid it. But it's the grain's natural starchiness that lends the luscious consistency. And, worst of all, many home cooks consider it too difficult to make. In reality, there's nothing hard about making risotto. It doesn't even require the constant stirring that's often part of the recipe. This version gets its flavor from homemade fish stock (page 134), good quality shrimp, and flavor-packed slow-roasted tomatoes. In fact, the tomatoes are flavorful enough to be the star of the dish in a vegetarian version that omits the shrimp and uses vegetable broth (page 137). **Serves 4 to 6**

Slow-Roasted Tomatoes

1 pound plum tomatoes, quartered and seeded

1 tablespoon olive oil, plus extra as needed

Kosher salt and freshly ground black pepper

Risotto

5 cups fish stock (page 134)

$1/2$ pound shrimp, peeled and deveined, cut into 1-inch pieces, shells and tails reserved

2 tablespoons butter, divided

$1/4$ cup minced shallots

$1^1/2$ cups Carnaroli or Arborio rice

$1/2$ cup dry white wine

$1/4$ cup loosely packed basil leaves, torn

Preheat the oven to 250°F. Line a rimmed baking sheet with aluminum foil.

TO MAKE THE TOMATOES, toss them with the oil and a pinch of salt and pepper. Transfer to the prepared sheet and roast in the oven for 3 hours. If you don't use the tomatoes right away, cool and then layer them in a small jar with 2 tablespoons oil. Cover and refrigerate up to one week.

TO PREPARE THE RISOTTO, heat the stock in a saucepan until simmering; add the shrimp shells and tails and simmer for 10 minutes. Strain, then return the stock to low heat to keep hot.

Melt 1 tablespoon of the butter over medium-high heat in a sauté pan. Add the shallots and cook, stirring occasionally, for 5 minutes, until softened but not starting to brown. Add the rice, stirring to combine with the butter and shallots for about 3 minutes, until the grains are coated in butter and the edges appear translucent. Add the wine and cook until almost absorbed, stirring occasionally.

Add about 1 cup of the hot stock and stir occasionally, for about 6 minutes. When the rice has absorbed most of the liquid, add another half-cup of stock. Keep adding stock in half-cup increments each time the risotto absorbs most of the liquid. Start tasting the rice for doneness when about a cup of stock remains. The risotto should look creamy and be tender with a little al dente bite—this takes about 30 minutes. When the risotto is almost done, add the sliced roasted tomatoes and shrimp; stir until the shrimp has just turned pink and cooked through, for no more than 2 minutes. Stir in the basil and the remaining 1 tablespoon butter (if desired) and season to taste just before serving. Drizzle with the tomato oil if you jarred them.

Shrimp and Pineapple Fried Rice

Tender bits of shrimp are completely at home in this sweet, spicy bed of rice. If you have a fish aversion, however, just sub thin slices of chicken or pork instead. Plus, with so many tasty elements at play in the base, you could easily omit any meat and the fish sauce to make it vegetarian friendly. Our rendition of fried rice negates the bad rap the dish has earned for being stir-fried in chunks of butter or oil. Instead of fat, tons of flavor from pineapple, ginger, garlic, and peppers cook up with chewy brown rice and umami-rich soy sauce. Skip takeout—this nourishing version in its pineapple bowl really delivers. **Serves 4**

1 large pineapple, cut in half lengthwise

2 tablespoons vegetable oil

$1/2$ small onion, cut into $1/4$-inch dice (about $1/2$ cup)

2 cloves garlic, minced (about 1 tablespoon)

1 (1-inch) piece fresh ginger, peeled and minced

1 small red bell pepper, cut into $1/4$-inch dice (about $1/2$ cup)

1 cup chopped sugar snap or snow peas

1 Thai chile, seeded and thinly sliced

2 tablespoons soy sauce

2 teaspoons fish sauce

4 cups cold cooked brown or white rice

$1/2$ pound shrimp, peeled, deveined, and cut into $1/4$-inch pieces

Make 2 bowls from the pineapple halves by carving out the center, leaving the bottom intact and leaving about a $1/2$-inch-thick border along the sides. Cut the carved out pineapple into small chunks, discarding the pieces of the tough center core. Set the pineapple shells and the chunks aside.

Coat a wok or a large sauté pan with the oil and set over medium-high heat. Once the oil is shimmering but not smoking, add the onion, garlic, ginger, bell pepper, peas, and chile. Stir-fry for about 2 minutes. Add the soy sauce, fish sauce, and rice, tossing to incorporate with the other ingredients. Add the shrimp, cooking just until done, for about 2 minutes. Remove from the heat and stir in the pineapple chunks. Spoon the rice into the carved out pineapple halves and serve.

FOUR TIPS FOR **SHRIMP SHOPPING**

Shopping for shrimp can be tricky, but these four tips will eliminate confusion and ensure delicious dishes.

DIY: You can buy shrimp that have been peeled, deveined, and cooked, but you'll pay a premium and the results won't taste that great. Instead, buy raw shrimp in the shell and peel, devein, and cook them yourself.

Frozen dinner: Unless you live very near where shrimp are caught, you are often better off buying frozen shrimp. Nonfrozen shrimp, though labeled fresh, have just been defrosted by your grocery store. It will actually be fresher if you thaw it yourself right before cooking.

Buy American: Much of the shrimp available to American shoppers has been pond raised in Asia, where regulations can be lax and food miles can be an issue. We recommend buying American shrimp where our recipes call for the sweet shellfish. In testing, we used frozen Florida pink shrimp with excellent results.

Buy by numbers: Terms like jumbo are not regulated. Instead of tag lines, seek out the count, which tells you how many of these shrimp it takes to make a pound. For example, U/15 shrimp are quite large—fewer than 15 of them weigh a pound ("U" stands for under). We like shrimp with counts around 21/25 (meaning from 21 to 25 of them will weigh one pound) for these recipes.

Crab Pad Thai

Whoever first declared haste makes waste must have been making pad Thai. While the dish actually comes together quickly, the key to highlighting its balance of sweet, salty, tart flavors and crunchy, soft, chewy textures is making it one serving at a time. Forcing all of the ingredients into the hot wok at once yields an indistinguishable sticky wad. Prepping all of the components—noodles, sauce, crab, vegetables, toppings—beforehand and setting them up alongside the stove makes for a speedy, multifaceted noodle dish. A half-pound of crab goes a long way. Add it at the end to prevent the tender lumps from shredding. For a vegetarian version, omit the crab, and add chunks of tofu (see opposite page for preparation instructions) to the wok with the noodles. Then swap 2 tablespoons of soy sauce and 2 tablespoons of lime juice for the fish sauce. **Serves 4**

8 ounces rice noodles

1 block tamarind pulp

$3^1/_2$ cups very hot water

$^1/_3$ cup fish sauce

3 tablespoons sugar

1 tablespoon soy sauce

8 teaspoons vegetable oil

2 cloves garlic, minced (about 1 tablespoon)

2 eggs, lightly beaten

8 ounces lump crabmeat

2 cups bean sprouts

6 scallions, white and green parts, thinly sliced

$^1/_2$ cup roasted salted peanuts, chopped

2 limes, cut into wedges, for serving

TO PREPARE THE NOODLES, place in a large bowl, cover with hot water, and soak for 15 minutes, until they've begun to soften. Rinse them under cold water and set aside.

TO PREPARE THE TAMARIND PASTE, break up the tamarind pulp in a bowl, cover with the $3^1/_2$ cups hot water, and soak for 20 minutes. With your fingers or a wooden spoon, mash the tamarind thoroughly into the water, separating the pods from the pulp. Push the mixture through a mesh strainer into another bowl, scraping the paste from the bottom of the strainer. This should yield approximately 2 1/4 cups paste. Measure 1 cup for this recipe. The remaining paste can be stored in an air-tight container or zippered storage bag in the refrigerator for several months or in the freezer indefinitely.

TO PREPARE THE SAUCE, whisk together the tamarind paste, fish sauce, sugar, and soy sauce in a bowl.

TO ASSEMBLE THE PAD THAI, make one serving at a time. Heat 2 teaspoons of the oil in a wok over high heat. When the wok and oil are very hot, drop in 2 cups of the noodles (loosely packed) and toss constantly for about 30 seconds. Add 1/4 cup of the sauce mixture and 1/2 teaspoon of minced garlic, tossing to coat the noodles. Push the noodles to one side and pour in 1/4 of the beaten eggs. Let the egg start to set up for a few seconds, and then scramble into the noodles. Add 1/4 each of the crabmeat, the bean sprouts, and the scallions. Toss quickly to heat all of the ingredients through. Transfer to a serving plate and sprinkle with some of the peanuts and more sprouts and scallions, if you like. Squeeze one lime wedge on the noodles and serve with one or two more. Repeat this process for the remaining servings. Rinse the wok with water to wipe out any caked on ingredients before starting again.

:tip: *Tamarind is a fruit that grows in pods on trees. Its seeds and pulp are used to add sweet and sour notes to dishes. Tamarind can be purchased in a few different forms, including paste, pulp, concentrate, and bricks of seeds and pulp. It can be found in Asian, Middle Eastern, and Indian markets, as well as the ethnic food aisles of some mainstream supermarkets.*

TOFU TIPS

If you've never worked with tofu before, it's important to know how to press it. Tofu is packed with water, and getting it as dry as possible is essential to making it taste good. The drier it is, the more readily it will absorb other flavors. Slice your tofu into 1-inch slabs and place between two clean, absorbent kitchen towels. Cover with a cutting board and something heavy, like your heaviest pot.

Leave it to press for at least one hour. After that, it's ready to use. Tofu is also one of the few foods whose texture actually benefits from freezing. Wrap your pressed slabs in plastic and place in a container for best results. After thawing overnight in the refrigerator, the tofu will cook up with an even meatier texture.

Corn and Cod Cakes

Crab cakes get all the glory, but many kinds of fish make terrific multi-ingredient patties. Fishcakes are part of the great thrifty tradition of stretching a small amount of an expensive ingredient. This one starts with cod, a versatile white fish. Be careful choosing cod: Pacific-caught is plentiful, but the overfishing of cod hailing from the Atlantic is causing destruction of ocean habitat. No Pacific cod at your market? Pacific sole, U.S.-farmed tilapia, and, yes, crab would all work well. **Serves 4 to 6**

Cod Cakes

$^1/_2$ pound cod fillet

1 tablespoon canola oil, plus 1 teaspoon

Salt and pepper

1 cup fresh or frozen corn kernels

1 large russet potato, peeled and cut into 1-inch chunks

$^1/_2$ tablespoon butter

1 slice thick-cut bacon, minced

1 roasted red bell pepper, cut into $^1/_4$-inch dice (about 1 cup)

$^1/_4$ small onion, minced (about $^1/_4$ cup)

1 egg, beaten

1 cup fresh bread crumbs

$^1/_4$ cup loosely packed fresh parsley leaves

Vinaigrette

1 tablespoon freshly squeezed lemon juice

$^1/_4$ cup extra virgin olive oil

1 tablespoon mayonnaise

1 tablespoon capers, minced

$^1/_8$ teaspoon salt

$^1/_8$ teaspoon freshly ground black pepper

Canola oil for pan frying the cakes

5 cups baby greens

TO MAKE THE COD CAKES, preheat the oven to 400°F. Oil a rimmed baking sheet.

Brush the cod with the 1 tablespoon canola oil, season with salt and pepper, and place on the prepared sheet. Toss the corn with the 1 teaspoon oil and a pinch of salt and pepper. Spread on a second rimmed sheet. Bake both for 8 minutes, or until the cod flakes easily. Set aside to cool.

Put the potato in cold salted water, bring to a boil, reduce the heat, and simmer for 10 minutes, or until fork-tender. Mash the potato and butter coarsely with a handheld masher.

Cook the bacon over medium heat for about 5 minutes, until the bacon is crisp and the fat has rendered. Transfer the bacon to a paper towel and set aside. Sauté the bell pepper and onion in the fat for 5 to 8 minutes, until softened. Add the corn and sauté for an additional 1 to 2 minutes (the corn tends to pop, so be careful). Allow to cool.

Beat the egg in a large bowl. Add the cod, potatoes, bacon, onion–corn–bell pepper mixture, bread crumbs, parsley, and salt and pepper to taste. Mix well. Use a $^1/_4$ cup dry measuring cup to form the mixture into $^1/_2$-inch-thick cakes. Refrigerate for at least one hour or up to one day.

TO MAKE THE VINAIGRETTE, whisk the lemon juice, olive oil, mayonnaise, capers, salt, and pepper together until emulsified. Taste for seasoning and adjust as needed. Set aside.

TO COOK THE COD CAKES, heat $^1/_4$ inch of canola oil in a frying pan over medium-high heat until shimmering but not smoking. Fry the cakes in batches, for about 3 minutes per side. Serve the cod cakes with or over baby greens with vinaigrette drizzled on top.

Fish, Bean, and Avocado Tacos

Fish tacos are a favorite on the West Coast, where morsels of fish are deep-fried for a crisp filling inside a soft tortilla. In this recipe, the fish is grilled, not fried, and paired with avocado salsa and vegetarian refried beans for a more nutritious version of the classic. Fresh, high-quality halibut and ripe, creamy avocados are key; as for the refried beans, feel free to take some help from your favorite brand in a can. **Serves 4**

Avocado Lime Salsa

2 ripe avocados, cut into $1/4$-inch dice

2 small tomatillos, cut into $1/4$-inch dice

1 medium tomato, cut into $1/4$-inch dice

1 jalapeño, seeded and minced

1 clove garlic, minced and mashed to a paste with $1/4$ teaspoon kosher salt

$1/4$ cup loosely packed fresh cilantro leaves, coarsely chopped

Zest and juice of $1/2$ lime

2 teaspoons olive oil

Kosher salt and freshly ground black pepper

Tacos

6 ounces halibut

2 teaspoons olive oil

$1/2$ teaspoon ground cumin

$1/2$ teaspoon chili powder

$1/2$ teaspoon kosher salt

Freshly ground black pepper

Juice of $1/2$ lime

8 soft taco flour or corn tortillas

1 (14-ounce) can vegetarian refried beans

4 ounces Oaxaca or cotija cheese, crumbled (optional)

Preheat the grill to medium heat.

TO MAKE THE SALSA, in a bowl, combine the avocado, tomatillos, tomato, jalapeño, garlic, cilantro, lime zest, lime juice, oil, and salt and pepper to taste. Set aside to let the flavors combine.

TO GRILL THE FISH, brush with oil on both sides and sprinkle with the cumin, chili powder, salt, and pepper. Grill each side for about 3 minutes. Remove the fish from the heat, cut into 1-inch chunks, and drizzle with the lime juice. Cover loosely with aluminum foil to keep warm and set aside. Lightly grill the tortillas to warm through and then cover with a kitchen towel to keep warm and soft.

Heat the refried beans in a small pot over medium heat, or microwave until soft and steaming, for about 2 minutes.

TO ASSEMBLE THE TACOS, spread a spoonful of warm beans on each tortilla and top with a few chunks of fish, a scoop of salsa, and cheese if you like. Alternatively, let diners build their own.

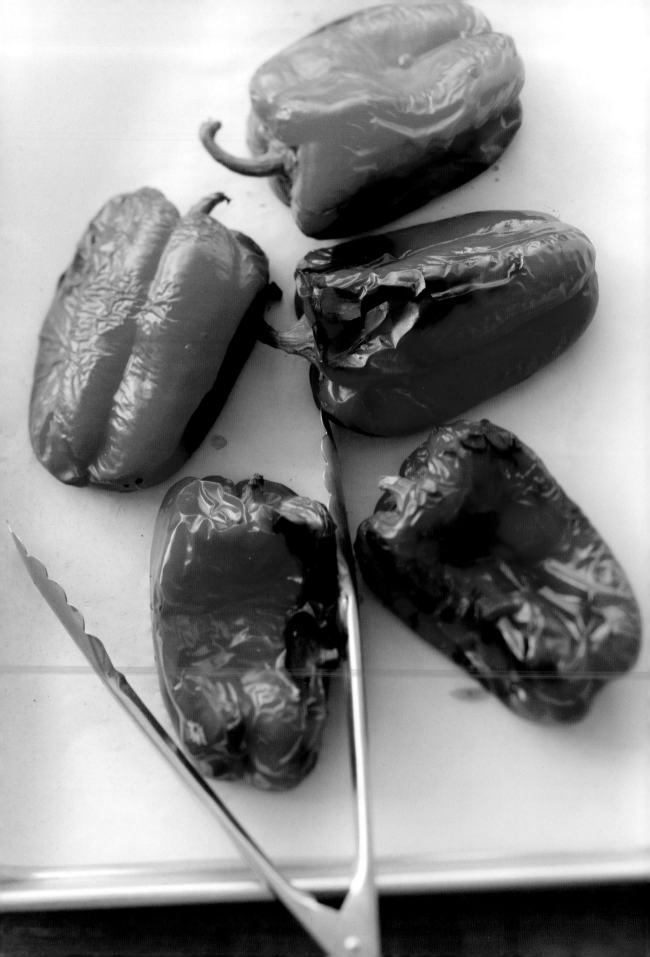

With a Little Less Pork

Americans like pork for good reason: applications for nearly every cut of this meat are simple and tasty.

We know a surprising number of vegetarians who make a special exception for bacon. With its fatty, smoky, salty taste and crunchy texture, it's pretty hard to resist as a partner for eggs or in a sandwich. Other vegetarians we know live with a similar exemption for Southern pulled pork sandwiches. It's easy to see why—these are some of the most delicious foods on the planet. On the other hand, the plight of the factory-farmed pig (and the communities who live near them) is hard to ignore. Breeding sows have it particularly hard, since many large producers confine them to small metal cages, known as gestation crates, too tiny to turn around in during pregnancy. But no pigs that live on these intensive operations get the basic components pigs need to be happy, like sunshine, grass, and ample space to move around in.

The good news for pigs is that the public is sympathetic. Due to pressure from consumers and environmental groups, Smithfield, the largest commercial pig farmer, has agreed to phase out gestation crates for pregnant sows during the next decade. The Mexican food chain restaurant Chipotle has a humane-pork-only policy and buys from reputable companies like Niman Ranch, a collective of small-scale farms dedicated to humane husbandry, and even smaller farms like Poly-face, the Virginia farm made famous in Michael Pollan's *The Omnivore's Dilemma*.

Niman Ranch products are available in regular groceries across the country. Farmers' markets also make humanely raised and heritage breeds of pork available to more shoppers every year. Restaurants will boast right on their menu when a dish is made from Berkshire pork, a heritage breed prized by chefs and gourmets for its rich flavor and higher fat content. But you can make the same quality meal at home by tracking down a source for humanely raised pork in your state. Online sources, like LocalHarvest.com, make it available to even those whose area is without a convenient farmers' market. Once you start working with these products in your own kitchen, you'll be amazed you ever settled for those commercially produced cuts. The flavor is so much better, and it's easy to limit the amount you use—some of our recipes use only 2 ounces of flavorful bacon to infuse a whole dish with a hearty, meaty personality.

Roasted Pork Shoulder

Pork shoulder is a good-sized piece of meat that can weigh upward of 7 pounds. Including it in a cookbook aimed at using less meat, then, seems contradictory. But tender, versatile pork shoulder is actually a perfect player in this type of cooking. It's relatively inexpensive and can be broken down into smaller portions. The meat freezes very well, before or after cooking. Most important, cooking pork shoulder is almost foolproof. Make this simple recipe when you have time for the slow roast, enjoy some of it immediately, and freeze the rest for quick meals later. This pork pairs beautifully with a number of sauces throughout the book and can stand in as the meat in other recipes, which we've called out on the opposite page. **Serves 8 to 10**

1 (5 to 7-pound) pork shoulder

Kosher salt and freshly ground black pepper

4 cloves garlic, coarsely chopped

2 tablespoons vegetable oil

$2\frac{1}{2}$ cups ham stock (page 136), chicken stock (page 131), or vegetable broth (page 137)

Preheat the oven to 350°F.

Season the pork shoulder with salt and pepper. Using a paring knife, poke about 10 small holes about $\frac{1}{4}$ inch deep across the top of the meat. Stick pieces of the chopped garlic in each hole.

Heat the oil in a large roasting pan on the stovetop over medium-high heat. When the pan is hot, sear the shoulder to brown the meat on all sides for a total of about 10 minutes. Lift the meat out of the pan and transfer to a plate. Add $\frac{1}{2}$ cup of the stock to the hot pan and scrape the bits off the bottom while the liquid sizzles. Put the meat back in the pan, add the rest of the stock, cover the pan with a lid or aluminum foil, and roast in the oven for about 3 hours, or until the meat shreds easily with a fork.

Remove the cover or foil from the pan, taking care to avoid a burst of steam. Ladle the liquid into a gravy separator or a bowl and cool slightly so the fat rises to the top of the liquid. Shred the pork with two forks. Return the defatted liquid to the pan, tossing with the meat. Use immediately, or cool and separate into smaller portions to freeze (wrap very well in plastic wrap or an air-tight container, label, and use within a few months).

Croccante Signore: The Crispy Mister

The *croque monsieur*, which translates to "crispy mister," is France's answer to the American grilled ham and cheese sandwich. We've given our version an Italian spin with aged prosciutto and smoky *caciocavallo* cheese. (Smoked mozzarella would be an excellent substitute.) Go with the pricy imported prosciutto. It's an artisanal product that's been produced with care in Italy for centuries. Just one ounce of the stuff provides a ton of satisfying flavor. A thin coating of mayo helps the sandwich fry up extra crunchy. For the bread, we like a soft, rustic Italian *boule*. **Serves 4**

8 (^{1}/$_2$-inch) slices good bakery bread

4 teaspoons Dijon mustard, or enough
    to spread on the inside of the
    sandwiches

4 ounces thinly sliced prosciutto

4 ounces smoked caciocavallo or other
    good melting cheese, grated

2 tablespoons mayonnaise, or enough
    to spread on the outside of the
    sandwiches

Preheat a cast iron or other heavy pan over medium-high heat for about 3 minutes.

Spread one slice of bread with mustard and layer on ^{1}/$_4$ of the prosciutto and ^{1}/$_4$ of the cheese. Top with another slice of bread, and spread a very thin layer of mayo on the outside of the sandwich, as you would butter the bread for a grilled cheese sandwich. Repeat with the remaining ingredients until you have 4 sandwiches. Place 2 sandwiches in your heated pan and do not disturb for 3 minutes, or until the cheese is beginning to melt and the bread is golden brown. Flip to brown the other side. Repeat with the other 2 sandwiches, making sure each rests for 5 minutes before cutting it. (If you cut them immediately, the cheese will run out of the sandwich.)

Antipasto Salad

We both grew up in households with kitchens under the Italian-American influence. Our family holiday dinners are almost always prefaced with antipasti spreads chock-full of meats, cheeses, and vegetables. This salad is inspired by those celebrations around the table and calls on sopressata, a favorite dried salami that is readily available in most Italian markets. Sopressata varies in diameter and flavor, so ask for a taste to find your favorite. Just a bit of its rich, meaty flavor and chewy texture goes a long way. Though we would be hard pressed to surrender this delicacy, the meatless version of our salad will attract the masses with as much fervor. Sweet roasted peppers, briny olives, and plump artichoke hearts blend with the vinaigrette destined for a mopping with a hunk of Italian bread. *Buon appetito!* **Serves 4 to 6**

1 head garlic

1 tablespoon olive oil

1 tablespoon water

2 red bell peppers

Balsamic Vinaigrette

2 tablespoons balsamic vinegar

$1/2$ teaspoon Dijon mustard

$1/2$ teaspoon honey

Pinch of kosher salt

4 tablespoons extra virgin olive oil

Salad

1 small head escarole, chopped or torn

1 small head red leaf lettuce, chopped or torn

2 ounces (sweet or hot) sliced sopressata, cut into small strips or chunks

$1/2$ cup thinly sliced red onion

$1/2$ cup chopped artichoke hearts

$1/3$ cup pitted Sicilian (or your favorite variety) olives, chopped

2 medium tomatoes, cut into $1/2$-inch dice, or $1/2$ cup slow-roasted tomatoes (page 52)

2 ounces provolone, cut into $1/4$-inch dice (about $1/4$ cup)

2 ounces mozzarella, cut into $1/4$-inch dice (about $1/4$ cup)

Freshly ground black pepper

Italian bread, sliced

TO ROAST THE GARLIC AND PEPPERS, preheat the oven to 450°F. Cut the head of garlic in half horizontally. Place on a piece of aluminum foil (about 6 inches long) and fold up the sides to make a vessel. Pour the olive oil and water over both halves of the garlic, and fold and pinch the foil sides, making a pouch to enclose the garlic. Transfer the garlic pouch and the 2 bell peppers to a rimmed baking sheet and into the oven. Roast for 45 minutes, turning a few times to blacken evenly.

When the garlic and peppers finish roasting, transfer the peppers to a bowl and cover with plastic wrap. Let them rest until they are cool enough to handle. Then peel and discard the blackened skins and slice them into strips. Let the garlic cool and then pop the cloves out of their skins.

TO MAKE THE VINAIGRETTE, whisk together the vinegar, mustard, honey, and a pinch of salt. Add the olive oil and whisk until an emulsion forms.

TO ASSEMBLE THE SALAD, toss the lettuces, sopressata, onion, artichoke hearts, olives, tomatoes, and cheeses together in a large bowl. Add the bell peppers and the garlic cloves. Drizzle the vinaigrette over the salad and toss to coat and combine. Season with freshly ground black pepper and serve on a large platter with slices of Italian bread.

Sausage and Pepper Sandwiches

Sausage and pepper sandwiches are right up there with burgers and dogs on the list of meaty crowd-pleasers. But you'll be surprised how far a mere half-pound of sausage goes in this version. Like its meatier cousin, though, these sandwiches aren't for neat freaks! Keep a plate under your chin to catch runaway veggies, sausage chunks, and delicious drips as you take a bite into this mildly spicy motley mix. Toss leftovers with hot cooked rigatoni and a bit of the water it was boiled in for a terrific pasta dish. **Serves 4 to 6**

2 small red bell peppers, cut into $1/2$-inch strips

1 large green bell pepper, cut into $1/2$-inch strips

1 medium yellow or white onion, cut into thin strips

8 ounces cremini mushrooms, cut in half

1 large fennel bulb, cut into $1/4$-inch strips

3 cloves garlic, coarsely chopped

$1/4$ cup dry red wine

$1/4$ cup olive oil

2 tablespoons balsamic vinegar

$1/4$ teaspoon dried chile flakes

1 teaspoon salt

$1/2$ teaspoon (about 20 grinds) freshly ground black pepper

$1/2$ pound hot Italian sausage, casings removed

4 to 6 soft Italian rolls, split lengthwise and lightly toasted

Freshly shaved Parmesan cheese

Preheat the oven to 375°F.

Mix the peppers, onion, mushrooms, and fennel in a 10 by 15-inch baking dish. In a bowl, whisk together the garlic, wine, oil, vinegar, chile flakes, salt, and pepper. Pour over the vegetables and toss to coat them well. Dot the top of the vegetables with small chunks of the sausage. Transfer to the oven and bake for about 40 minutes, or until the sausage is cooked and the vegetables have softened but have retained a slight bite. Stir once halfway through.

When the sausage and peppers come out of the oven, push them to one side of the dish and carefully tip the juices to the other end. Open the rolls and dunk them quickly, face down, to sop up some of the juice (not so much that the bread gets soggy). Fill each roll with several spoonfuls of the sausage and peppers and top with cheese.

Lentil Soup

Rustic and forgiving, lentil soup should be one of the first dishes in any aspiring cook's repertoire. This recipe yields delicious results but could easily be modified a dozen ways. No sausage? Use bacon instead. Not crazy about fennel? Just leave it out. Prefer a completely creamy texture? Blend the whole soup instead of just a third. If you have an afternoon to dedicate to soup making, we suggest letting the onion, celery, carrots, and fennel cook over low heat for up to 90 minutes. Doing so changes their individual flavors into a single background note that adds amazing depth and complexity to the dish. But when you're short on time, cook them for just 10 minutes. It will still be much better than anything you'd find in a can. **Serves 4**

1 tablespoon olive oil

4 ounces hot Italian sausage, casings removed

1 small onion, cut into $1/4$-inch dice

1 red bell pepper, cut into $1/4$-inch dice (about 1 cup)

2 stalks celery, cut into $1/4$-inch dice (about $1/2$ cup)

2 carrots, cut into $1/4$-inch dice (about 1 cup)

1 small fennel bulb, cut into $1/4$-inch dice (about 1 cup)

Kosher salt and freshly ground black pepper

1 tablespoon tomato paste

3 cloves garlic, minced

1 cup crushed tomatoes

$1^1/_2$ cups brown lentils

6 cups water

3 (2-inch) Parmesan cheese rinds

1 bay leaf

1 cup grated Parmesan or Romano cheese (4 ounces), plus extra for serving

1 tablespoon balsamic vinegar

Good-quality artisanal bread, for serving

Extra virgin olive oil, for drizzling

Put the 1 tablespoon olive oil in a Dutch oven over medium heat. Add the sausage, breaking up with a spoon, and cook for about 10 minutes, until the fat is rendered and the sausage is well browned. Remove the sausage bits, and set aside.

Add the onion, bell pepper, celery, carrots, fennel, and 1 teaspoon salt. Adjust the heat to medium and cook, stirring occasionally, for at least 10 minutes, or until the vegetables are softened.

Add the tomato paste, stirring well to coat the vegetables, and cook for about 2 minutes to melt the paste. Add the garlic, tomatoes, lentils, water, cheese rinds, and bay leaf. Turn the heat to high, bring to a boil, and then reduce the heat to medium-low. Simmer for 30 minutes. Remove and discard the bay leaf and cheese rinds.

Place the 1 cup cheese in a blender. Add about one-third of the soup to the blender and puree the soup and cheese, making sure your blender is less than $1/3$ full. Return the puree to the pot, add the reserved sausage bits, stir to combine, and add the balsamic vinegar. Taste for seasoning, adding salt and pepper if desired. Serve with bread, additional grated Parmesan, and a drizzle of extra virgin olive oil.

Lyonnaise Salad

This underappreciated bistro classic provides a perfect example of meat in moderation. Crisp bacon pieces, called *lardons* in France, provide the perfect foil for the soft texture of a runny poached egg. Lacy frisée helps capture bacon bits, eggy bites, and tart vinaigrette in every forkful. Unlike so many salads that provide little in the way of protein, this balanced dish is the kind of lunch that can power a long afternoon. Paired with a glass of wine, it's also a delicious but easy dinner. **Serves 4**

1 medium russet potato, cut into $1/4$-inch dice

5 tablespoons olive oil, divided

Salt and freshly ground black pepper

2 slices bacon, cut into $1/4$-inch dice

$1/2$ small shallot, minced

$1^1/2$ teaspoons Dijon mustard

2 tablespoons Champagne vinegar or other white wine vinegar

1 head frisée, torn into bite-size pieces (about 4 cups)

1 tablespoon white wine vinegar

4 eggs

Preheat the oven to 400°F. Lightly oil a rimmed baking sheet.

In a bowl, combine the potatoes with 2 tablespoons of the oil and season with salt and pepper. Spread the potatoes on the prepared baking sheet, and roast for about 30 minutes, until golden brown and crisp. Set aside to cool slightly.

While the potatoes are cooking, fry the bacon over medium heat until crisp. Drain and set aside. For the dressing, combine the shallot, mustard, vinegar, and remaining 3 tablespoons oil in a jar with a secure lid and shake until emulsified.

While the potatoes are cooling, toss the frisée with the dressing in a large bowl; divide into four portions on plates.

Fill a 10-inch, straight-sided pan with $1^1/2$ inches of water (or use a Dutch oven or other large sauce pot). Add the vinegar and bring the liquid to a bare simmer, so that there are active bubbles, but the water is not rolling. Gently crack the eggs one by one, slipping them into the water and taking care not to break the yolks (you may need to do this in batches, depending on the size of your pan). Run a spoon through the water to prevent the eggs from sticking to the bottom. Reduce the heat to low and let the eggs cook for 3 to 5 minutes, or until the whites have set and the yolk is done to the desired consistency, and remove with a slotted spoon. Blot the bottom of the spoon on a kitchen towel to catch the draining water. Place an egg on each portion of frisée, sprinkling the bacon bits and potato croutons evenly over each portion, and sprinkle with salt and pepper to taste.

Potato Corn Chowder

The best chowders are rich with a strong undercurrent of smoky pork flavor. This recipe achieves both of those things, but amazingly with just 2 slices of bacon and not a drop of cream. Here, we marshal the awesome power of bacon and silken tofu for a wholesome and hearty soup that's as thick as traditional chowder but without the excess fat and calories of a cream-based dish. Don't tell your friends and family about the tofu until they've licked their bowls clean. For a vegan version, omit the bacon, substitute 2 tablespoons nutritional yeast for the Parmesan cheese rind, swap vegetable broth (page 137) for the chicken stock, and season with smoked salt. **Serves 4 to 6**

2 slices bacon, cut into ¼-inch dice	1 pound Yukon gold potatoes, peeled and cut into ½-inch dice
6 ounces silken tofu	4 cups chicken stock (page 131)
5 cups fresh or frozen corn kernels	1 bay leaf
Salt and pepper	3 (2-inch) pieces Parmesan cheese rind
1 medium onion, cut into ¼-inch dice	1 small bunch chives, minced

Cook the bacon in a Dutch oven or large saucepot over medium heat for about 5 to 7 minutes, until the fat renders and the bacon is crisp. Remove the bacon bits from the pot and set aside.

While the bacon is cooking, combine the tofu with 2 cups of the corn and ½ teaspoon salt in a food processor and puree until smooth and creamy. Set aside.

Add the onion to the bacon fat left in the pot, and cook over medium heat, stirring occasionally, for about 10 minutes, until the onion is completely softened but not brown.

Add the potatoes and the remaining 3 cups corn, along with a heavy pinch of salt and a few grinds of pepper, and stir to combine. Add the stock, bay leaf, and cheese rind, bring the liquid to a boil, and then reduce the heat; let the soup simmer for 20 minutes, until the potatoes are very tender. Remove the cheese rind and bay leaf.

Working in batches, puree about half the soup in a blender or food processor. (Or blend partially with a stick blender in the pot.) Return the pureed soup to the pot and stir in the pureed tofu and corn mixture. Simmer for 10 more minutes. Taste for salt and pepper and adjust as needed. Top with chives and reserved bacon bits.

Tomato Pancetta Linguine

This dish is a hearty match between basic pasta and flavor-packed bacon that is simple to prepare but complex in flavor. Pancetta starts the sauce, aromatic with garlic and rosemary, and tops off the entire dish as bits of savory crunch. You can substitute bacon if you can't find pancetta or if you prefer the smoky dimension that unsmoked pancetta lacks. Either way, don't hesitate to grate on extra Parmesan cheese! **Serves 4 to 6**

4 ounces (about 4 slices) pancetta or bacon, chopped into $1/4$-inch bits	1 (28-ounce) can peeled tomatoes, chopped, juice reserved
1 large shallot, coarsely chopped	$1/2$ teaspoon sugar (optional)
2 cloves garlic, sliced thin lengthwise	Salt and freshly ground black pepper (optional)
$1/2$ teaspoon chopped fresh rosemary leaves	1 pound dried linguine
$1/4$ cup dry white wine	Freshly grated Parmesan cheese
1 tablespoon sherry vinegar	

Add the pancetta to a hot, dry sauté pan over medium-high heat. Cook for about 3 minutes, until crisp. Transfer the pancetta bits from the pan to a paper towel and reserve. Add the shallot to the pancetta fat in the hot pan and sauté for about 3 minutes, until soft and fragrant. Add the garlic and rosemary, sautéing for another 30 seconds. Pour in the wine and vinegar, scraping the bottom until most of the liquid has cooked out. Add the tomatoes (including juices) and simmer for 20 minutes. Taste for seasoning and add the sugar if the sauce is too tart, and salt and pepper if necessary.

Meanwhile, cook the linguine according to the package directions. Just before draining the pasta, add $1/2$ cup of the pasta water to the tomato sauce. Toss the hot, drained pasta with the tomato sauce. Sprinkle with pancetta bits and cheese and serve.

Barley Pilaf Stuffed Squash

Barley is a common ingredient in hearty dishes like soup, stew, and stuffing. Here the grain is the base of a pilaf-like filling for soft roasted butternut squash. The minimal amount of sweet Italian sausage marries beautifully with fragrant sage and chewy tart cranberries, but if you're going veggie, just omit it. Woodsy porcini mushrooms are meaty enough to carry the dish. Depending on size, each squash can be an individual serving, or 2 large halves can be stuffed and divided.

Serves 4

2 small butternut squash, or 1 large squash, halved, seeds scooped out

1 tablespoon plus 2 teaspoons olive oil

Kosher salt and freshly ground black pepper

$1/3$ cup (about $1/2$ ounce) dried porcini mushrooms

3 cups hot water

1 cup barley

2 teaspoons olive oil

4 ounces sweet Italian sausage (or your favorite flavor)

2 cloves garlic, minced (about 1 tablespoon)

1 small shallot, minced

1 tablespoon chopped fresh sage (about 4 large leaves)

$1/4$ cup dried cranberries, chopped

2 tablespoons balsamic vinegar

$1/2$ cup toasted pecans, chopped

Preheat the oven to 375°F.

TO PREPARE THE SQUASH, rub the insides with the 1 tablespoon oil, salt, and pepper, and transfer to a large roasting pan that will fit all the pieces without crowding. Roast in the oven, cut side down, for 45 minutes to 1 hour, until the squash is fork tender.

Meanwhile, **TO PREPARE THE FILLING**, let the mushrooms steep in the hot water in a medium saucepan for about 15 minutes. Remove the rehydrated mushrooms, chop, and set aside. Bring the soaking water to a boil, add the barley, and simmer for about 30 minutes, until the barley is cooked through.

While the barley cooks, add the 2 teaspoons oil to a sauté pan over medium-high heat. Cut and remove the sausage casings and crumble the meat into the pan. Cook the sausage until it begins to brown, stirring occasionally. Add the garlic, shallot, sage, cranberries, and reserved mushrooms and cook for another 2 minutes.

Drain the barley through a mesh strainer and add to the sausage pan. Add the vinegar and stir to combine thoroughly with the rest of the ingredients. Season to taste with salt and pepper. Keep warm until the squash is ready.

When the squash is done, remove from the oven and stuff the craters with the hot barley mixture. Sprinkle with toasted pecans and serve.

Posole Burritos with Escabèche Slaw

Posole is a traditional Mexican soup/stew, long simmered and rich with pork and hominy. A genuine posole is made with a pig's head, but we found a more approachable alternative in pork tenderloin, a great source of lean protein, vitamins, and minerals. Hominy is dried white or yellow corn kernels from which the hull and germ have been removed. **Serves 4 to 6**

Escabèche Slaw

$1/2$ teaspoon salt

$1/2$ teaspoon sugar

3 tablespoons red wine vinegar

3 cups shredded cabbage or bagged coleslaw mix

1 cup thinly sliced red onion

Posole

1 dried guajillo, pasilla, or New Mexican red chile

1 cup hot water

4 teaspoons vegetable oil, divided

3 small tomatillos, cut into $1/4$-inch dice

1 small onion, cut into $1/4$-inch dice

2 cloves garlic, smashed and peeled

2 teaspoons ground coriander, divided

2 teaspoons ground cumin, divided

1 (28-ounce) can crushed tomatoes

2 cups dried hominy, cooked, or 1 (15-ounce) can, drained and rinsed

1 teaspoon ancho chile powder

$1/4$ teaspoon salt

8 ounces pork tenderloin, cut into $1/2$-inch cubes

$1/4$ cup water

Burritos

8 to 12 (10- or 12-inch) corn or flour tortillas

1 cup loosely packed fresh cilantro leaves, coarsely chopped

Sour cream (optional)

Shredded cheddar or pepper jack cheese (optional)

TO MAKE THE SLAW, whisk the salt and sugar into the vinegar in a large bowl. Add the cabbage and onion and toss well. Cover the bowl and let rest in the refrigerator for at least 30 minutes. Taste for seasoning and adjust as needed. The slaw can be made up to a day ahead.

TO MAKE THE POSOLE, place a Dutch oven over medium-high heat and add the chile. Toast the chile for about 10 minutes, turning a few times. Remove from the pan, trim off the stem, scrape out the seeds, and soak in the hot water for about 15 minutes.

Meanwhile, heat 2 teaspoons of the oil in the same pot. Add the tomatillos, onion, and garlic. Sauté for about 5 minutes before stirring in 1 teaspoon coriander, 1 teaspoon cumin, the tomatoes, and the hominy. Add the rehydrated chile and the soaking water. Simmer for about 15 minutes.

Add the remaining 2 teaspoons vegetable oil to a separate sauté pan over medium-high heat. Mix the remaining coriander and cumin with the chile powder and salt and rub it into the pork cubes. When the oil is hot, add the pork and cook for about 2 minutes, to brown slightly. Scrape the pork into the simmering hominy mixture. Add the $1/4$ cup water and scrape up any bits. Pour into the pot with the other ingredients. Simmer for 10 minutes. Adjust seasoning as needed.

TO ASSEMBLE THE BURRITOS, warm the tortillas over a gas flame just until they are flecked with charred spots, or heat them in a 250°F oven, stacked and wrapped in foil, for 15 minutes. Put about $1/4$ cup of the hot posole mixture in the center of a tortilla. Top with a spoonful of slaw, a sprinkle of chopped cilantro, a dollop of sour cream, and a scatter of cheese. Wrap like a burrito.

Red Beans and Rice

Red beans and rice is a New Orleans tradition that was historically made on Mondays, putting to use the ham left over from Sunday dinner. Recipes are as varied as the crowd at Mardi Gras, but almost all of them call for the holy trinity, New Orleans's version of the aromatic base mirepoix—bell peppers, onions, and celery. There is nothing complicated about our version of the classic, but its flavors, from just a bit of spicy andouille sausage and smoky ham, are complex, and its creamy bean and rice textures are so very satisfying. **Serves 4 to 6**

2 teaspoons vegetable oil

3 ounces (about 1 link) andouille sausage

1/4 pound cooked ham, chopped into
    1/4-inch pieces

1 small onion, cut into 1/4-inch dice (about
    1 cup)

1 small green bell pepper, cut into 1/4-inch
    dice (about 1/2 cup)

2 stalks celery, cut into 1/4-inch dice (about
    1/2 cup)

2 cloves garlic, minced (about 1 tablespoon)

1/4 teaspoon cayenne pepper

3 cups dried kidney beans, cooked, or
    2 (15-ounce) cans, drained and rinsed

2 sprigs thyme

1 bay leaf

4 cups ham stock (page 136)

1 1/2 cups long-grain rice

2 cups water

Salt and pepper

TO COOK THE BEANS, heat the oil in a Dutch oven over medium-high heat. Cut or crumble the sausage into small pieces and add to the pot once the oil is hot. Cook the sausage for about 5 minutes, until it begins to brown. Add the ham, onion, pepper, and celery and sauté for an additional 2 minutes. Stir in the garlic and cayenne, and cook for about 30 seconds, until fragrant. Add the beans, thyme, bay leaf, and 3 cups of the stock. Bring to a boil and then reduce the heat to medium-low. Simmer for at least 30 minutes, until the liquid begins to thicken as the beans break down.

Meanwhile, **TO COOK THE RICE,** bring the remaining ham stock and the water to a boil in a medium saucepan. Add the rice and let the liquid return to a boil. Cover the pot and reduce the heat to low. Cook the rice for 25 minutes, then turn off the heat and let it sit without lifting the cover, for another 5 to 10 minutes. Fluff the cooked rice with a fork and season with salt and pepper.

TO FINISH THE DISH AND SERVE IT UP, when the bean mixture has simmered and thickened, remove the thyme sprigs and bay leaf and season with salt and pepper as needed. Transfer the hot rice to a large serving platter and top with the bean mixture.

Sweet Potato Chorizo Mole

Chorizo, a spicy pork sausage made with garlic and chiles, is available both fresh and cured. Either works well in this recipe. (If you use cured chorizo, cut it into pieces rather than crumbling into the pan.) The smooth, rich tomato sauce is inspired by traditional mole sauce, which typically gets some of its depth from the addition of bittersweet chocolate. **Serves 4 to 6**

2 teaspoons vegetable oil

4 ounces (about 2 links) chorizo sausage

$1/2$ small onion, cut into $1/4$-inch dice (about $1/2$ cup)

2 cloves garlic, minced (about 1 tablespoon)

2 teaspoons chopped fresh oregano leaves, or 1 teaspoon dried

1 (28-ounce) can whole peeled tomatoes, juices strained and reserved, tomatoes chopped

$1^1/2$ teaspoons ground cumin

1 tablespoon ancho chile powder

1 ounce bittersweet chocolate, chopped (about 2 tablespoons)

1 cup fresh or frozen corn, or 1 (11-ounce) can, drained

$1^1/2$ cups dried black beans, cooked, or 1 (15-ounce) can, drained and rinsed

$2/3$ cup water

Kosher salt and freshly ground black pepper

$1^1/2$ pounds yellow or orange sweet potatoes, peeled and cut lengthwise into $1/8$ inch slices, or in disks

8 ounces Cheddar cheese, shredded

1 avocado, sliced, for garnish

2 limes, cut into wedges, for garnish

Cilantro sprigs for garnish

Preheat the oven to 375°F. Brush a 9 by 13-inch baking dish lightly with oil.

TO PREPARE THE TOMATO MIXTURE, heat the oil in a large skillet over medium-high heat. Slice the surface of the sausages lengthwise to remove the meat from the casings. Crumble the meat into the hot pan and sauté for about 5 minutes, breaking it up further as it cooks and begins to brown. Add the onion and sauté for 2 minutes. Add the garlic and oregano and cook for 30 seconds more.

Pour the reserved tomato juices into the pan to deglaze, scraping the bits from the bottom. Add the chopped tomatoes, cumin, chile powder, and chocolate. Stir to combine while the chocolate melts. Add the corn and black beans, reduce the heat to medium, and allow the mixture to simmer for about 10 minutes. Stir in the water. Taste for seasoning and add salt and pepper if necesary.

Meanwhile, **TO ASSEMBLE AND COOK**, spread one-third of the sweet potatoes on the bottom of the prepared baking dish, overlapping the slices. Scoop half the tomato mixture (a heaping cup) and spread evenly across the first layer of potatoes. Top with one-third of the shredded cheese. Repeat this layering process, ending with a layer of potatoes. Reserve the last third of the cheese.

Once assembled, cover with foil, pushing it onto the surface of the top layer, and bake for 1 to $1^1/2$ hours, until potatoes are fork tender (yellow sweet potatoes tend to take longer). Remove the foil and sprinkle the remaining third of the cheese atop the potatoes. Bake for an additional 10 minutes.

Remove from the oven and let rest for at least 10 minutes to allow the layers to set up.

Cut and serve with avocado and lime wedges. Garnish with cilantro as desired.

:tip: *Use a mandoline or food processor slicing disk for easy, even slicing of the sweet potatoes.*

Pork Pot Stickers

Pot stickers are an excellent appetizer option that can also be made into a meal with the addition of fried rice or a bowl of sweet and sour soup. This recipe is full of flavor from earthy cabbage and mushrooms, crunchy carrots, and fragrant cilantro. With or without the pork, these crisp-tender dumplings are a crowd pleaser. The filling can be made and refrigerated up to two days ahead, and the pot stickers can be assembled, stored on a baking sheet, covered, and refrigerated for several hours. **Serves 8 to 10 as an appetizer (makes 40 pot stickers)**

3 tablespoons plus 2 teaspoons vegetable oil

4 ounces ground pork

2 tablespoons minced fresh ginger

3 tablespoons sliced scallion, white and green parts

2 cloves garlic, minced (about 1 tablespoon)

1 cup chopped mushrooms (about 4 ounces)

$1/4$ savoy cabbage, cored and cut into thin ribbons, then coarsely chopped (about 1 cup)

1 small carrot, shredded (about $1/2$ cup)

1 teaspoon rice wine vinegar

2 tablespoons soy sauce

$1/3$ cup loosely packed fresh cilantro or Thai basil leaves, chopped

$1/2$ teaspoon dark (Asian) sesame oil

1 teaspoon kosher salt

Freshly ground black pepper

40 wonton wrappers

1 cup chicken stock (page 131)

2 teaspoons toasted sesame seeds (optional)

TO MAKE THE FILLING, heat the 2 teaspoons vegetable oil in a large skillet over medium-high heat. Add the pork and cook for about 3 minutes, stirring to break the meat up into small bits. Add the ginger, scallion, and garlic and sauté for about 1 minute. Mix in the mushrooms, cabbage, and carrot and cook until the liquid released from the vegetables evaporates. Remove the mixture from the heat and add the vinegar, soy sauce, cilantro, sesame oil, salt, and pepper to taste, mixing well to incorporate the ingredients. Let cool slightly, or cover and refrigerate until ready to assemble.

TO ASSEMBLE THE POT STICKERS, put 1 teaspoon of the filling in the center of a wonton wrapper. Paint the edges of the wrapper with water. If you are using round wrappers, fold into a half circle, pressing the sides together. If you are using small rectangular wrappers, fold in half into a triangle and then fold the two side points in to the center, forming a little envelope-shaped package. Cover the assembled pot stickers with a damp cloth to prevent drying while forming the rest.

TO COOK THE POT STICKERS, heat 1 tablespoon of the vegetable oil in the skillet over medium-high heat. Working in batches, add 8 to 10 pot stickers to the hot pan, frying for about 3 minutes for a brown, crusty bottom. Pour $1/4$ cup stock into the pan and cover for about 30 seconds or until the liquid has evaporated, lifting the pot stickers from the bottom of the pan. Transfer the batch to a rimmed baking sheet and hold in a warm oven (about 200°F). Repeat the procedure with the remaining pot stickers, adding oil to the skillet as needed.

TO SERVE, transfer the pot stickers to a platter and sprinkle with the sesame seeds if you like.

Beef in Moderation

A little beef from the right source adds rich flavor, texture, and sustenance to old standbys as well as creative new dishes.

The USDA estimates that the average American eats 67 pounds of beef per year. And who can blame us? It's an edible American icon that's essential to our back-yard barbecues and holiday tables. But beneath the buns and bordelaise sauce lies meat from cows that probably lived very unhappy lives.

Cows were meant to roam a field and eat grass, but the majority of American beef and dairy cows are raised in Concentrated Animal Feeding Operations (CAFOs). The goal of these facilities is to produce more meat (or milk) in less time, in order to supply fast food empires and maintain the low prices Americans demand. CAFO animals are forced to grow at supernatural rates, courtesy of growth hormone injections and a grain-based diet composed mostly of corn. But cows aren't equipped with the enzymes required to break down grains so their CAFO diet is actually toxic.

In addition to the acidosis spurred by food that cow stomachs can't digest, animals are stuffed in cages with hundreds, sometimes thousands of others, in unsanitary conditions, and then given antibiotics to ward off disease. It is arguable that doses of antibiotics given to cows, which end up becoming our dinner, are causing human immunity to antibiotics for our own diseases.

Lucky for you, the consumer, and for us, the authors of a cookbook about meat, there are appetizing alternatives to commodity beef from this hapless herd. Pasture-raised animals eat the food they were meant to digest—good ol' grass—and are not pumped with growth hormones to speed the process. (It takes nearly twice as long for pasture-raised beef to reach slaughter maturity.) They also carry out their days in open fields, their natural habitat, rather than in crowded feedlots. Since disease is less likely to run rampant in this environment, and because the animals' systems are not subject to disruption from supplements, antibiotics are not commonplace.

Grass varies, which means that the flavor and texture of grass-fed beef can vary just as much. For Americans accustomed to factory-farmed, corn-gorged beef, grass-fed beef can be an acquired taste. But meat from grass-fed cows that are moving around on pasture is also much leaner and lower in saturated fat than from sedentary grain-fed cows (and milk from grass-fed cows is reported to be more nutrient rich). This leaner beef should be cooked lower and slower than grain fed (120°F to 140°F as opposed to 145°F to 170°F prescribed by USDA) to prevent drying.

Marketing terms can make choosing beef confusing. Buy from a trustworthy and informative source who will guide you through your options. Ask for beef that is antibiotic and hormone free, from cows that were fed a grass-based diet outside of confinement. While pasture-raised beef is more expensive, the grass is greener on the other side of the CAFO walls for cows, the earth, and consumers.

TERMS TO REMEMBER

Organic beef is from cows that have been raised on 100 percent organic feed, not necessarily grass. They must be given access to pasture and cannot receive growth hormones or antibiotics, but they can be confined to feedlots. USDA standards for "grass-fed" allow some confinement to feedlots, antibiotics, and growth hormones provided the diet is entirely grass and hay, not grain. Confinement to feedlots is also not banned under the USDA "Naturally Raised" terminology. The American Grassfed Association is developing a certification program that employs stricter parameters, requiring a grass-based diet and banning any confinement, medication, or hormones.

ABOUT BEANS

Canned beans are a nutritious part of this and many other recipes. And for convenience, they can't be beaten. But legume enthusiasts know that what you save in time you lose in flavor and texture. Cooking beans from dried can take hours, even after you've thought ahead and soaked them overnight. One possible way to get the best-tasting beans into a recipe faster is to cook them in a pressure cooker. These devices cook the beans to perfection in a fraction of the time. Today's models are safe, quiet, and useful for anyone pressed for time. Follow the manufacturer's directions for cooking different types of beans.

Beefed-Up Bean Chili

An age-old debate about "authentic" chili calls into question the inclusion of beans in the recipe. Self-proclaimed die-hards argue only the meatiest, beanless batch is the real deal, while countless delicious recipes offer bean-filled alternatives. This version is one of them, complete with three beans and meat (just exclude the beef for a vegetarian version). Peanuts, like black beans and kidney beans, are legumes. Peanut butter serves as the third bean, imparting a velvety mouthfeel and rich dimension as it melts into the tomato base. Call it what you want—we bet you'll like it enough to consider it a bona fide chili favorite. **Serves 4 to 6**

1 dried ancho or guajillo chile

1 tablespoon vegetable oil

4 ounces lean ground beef

1 small white onion, cut into $1/4$-inch dice (about 1 cup)

3 cloves garlic, minced

1 jalapeño, seeded and chopped

3 tablespoons smooth natural peanut butter

1 (28-ounce) can crushed tomatoes

$1/2$ cup loosely packed fresh cilantro leaves, chopped

1 tablespoon unsweetened cocoa powder

3 teaspoons ground cumin

2 tablespoons chili powder

1 tablespoon cider vinegar

$1/2$ cup water

$1\frac{1}{2}$ cups dried pinto beans, cooked, or 1 (15-ounce) can, drained and rinsed

$1\frac{1}{2}$ cups dried kidney beans, cooked, or 1 (15-ounce) can, drained and rinsed

2 teaspoons kosher salt

Freshly ground black pepper

Chopped scallions, shredded cheddar cheese, and sour cream for garnish

Heat a Dutch oven or a large pot over medium-high heat. Add the dried pepper and toast for 5 minutes, turning once or twice. Move the pepper to a bowl and cover it with hot water. Soak for about 15 minutes, to rehydrate and soften. Remove from the water, cut off the stem, scrape out the seeds, and chop.

Add the oil to the Dutch oven over medium-high heat. When the oil is hot, brown the beef for about 3 minutes, stirring occasionally to break it up into small pieces. Add the onion, garlic, jalapeño, and rehydrated chile and cook for an additional 5 minutes. Stir in the peanut butter and continue mixing until it melts. Add the tomatoes, cilantro, cocoa powder, cumin, chili powder, vinegar, $1/2$ cup water, and beans. Reduce the heat to low and simmer uncovered for about 45 minutes. Season with the salt and pepper to taste. Ladle the chili into bowls and serve with your choice of toppings; we like scallions, cheddar, and sour cream.

The B4 (Beef Bulgur Bean Burger)

We took on an almost meatless burger as a challenge to ourselves. A hamburger, after all, crowns the list of Ultimate Meat dishes. When Tara's husband, a guy from Oklahoma whose favorite food is a cheeseburger from a revered hamburger joint in Tulsa, said "I'd order this over a regular burger," we knew we had pulled it off! Bulgur wheat factors in 5 grams of fiber per serving, and its textured chew is complementary to a variety of dishes, including, as it turns out, a burger. **Serves 6**

1 cup dried black beans, cooked, or
    1 (15-ounce) can, drained and rinsed

1 clove garlic, minced and mashed to a
    paste with $1/4$ teaspoon kosher salt

3 scallions, white and green parts, minced

1 tablespoon whole-grain mustard

1 cup chicken stock (page 131) or water

$1/2$ cup coarse- or medium-grind bulgur
    wheat

$1/4$ teaspoon kosher salt

$1/4$ teaspoon freshly ground black pepper

1 egg, lightly beaten

8 ounces ground beef

6 hamburger buns (whole grain
    recommended)

Fixings of your choice, such as lettuce,
    sliced tomato, and sliced onion

Preheat the grill to medium-high and lightly oil the grates.

Pulse the beans, garlic paste, scallions, and mustard several times in a food processor until a chunky paste forms. (Alternatively, mash the beans and the other ingredients well with a fork or potato masher.) Transfer the mixture to a large bowl and set aside.

Bring the stock to a boil in a small saucepan. Stir in the bulgur wheat, cover, and reduce the heat. Simmer for 15 minutes. Remove from the heat, fluff with a fork. Season with the salt and pepper, or to taste, and let cool slightly.

Add the egg, bulgur wheat, and beef to the bean mixture and stir to combine the ingredients evenly. Form into 6 equal patties, about 4 ounces and $1/2$ inch thick each. You can make 4 jumbo burgers (6 ounces each) or 10 sliders (2.5 ounces each).

Grill the burgers over a medium-high flame for about 5 to 7 minutes per side. Transfer from the grill to hamburger buns and top with your favorite fixings. Alternatively, the burgers can be pan-fried over medium-high heat in a lightly oiled nonstick pan.

BURGER TIME

There are myriad ways to cut down on the beef in your burger. Our burger incorporates bulgur to boost fiber and cut some beef. A half turkey, half beef sandwich would likely fool your dinner guests. Tofu would also mesh well with all but the leanest ground beef. Minced mushrooms and even shredded beets have an earthy quality that's a natural fit in burgers. Moisture from vegetables can also keep patties from drying out on the grill. Some swear by surprising secret ingredients like cherries, nuts, or grated apples. Experiment, and you just might discover a new mix that is not only better for you but tastier too.

Caramelized Onion Meat Loaf

We know. Meat loaf evokes images of bland dinners off the kitchen tables of black and white television shows. And the words "meat" and "loaf" molded together as a pair are unappealing. OK, and sometimes meat loaf doesn't even *look* delicious. But the colorful tastes of this beef and tofu (give it a chance, meat lovers) combo, boosted by caramelized onions and a tangy sweet glaze, will surprise you as much as if Beaver Cleaver used "colorful" language at supper. Crumbled tofu takes on the flavors and textures of hearty ground beef and drastically cuts the fat content of this classic. The recipe serves a good number of folks, so make it for a crowd, or have a loaf of soft white bread on hand for sandwiches later in the week. One bite and you'll be piling on the mashed potatoes and buttered peas while waving an American flag. **Serves 6 to 8**

1 tablespoon bacon fat, vegetable oil, or butter

1 tablespoon vegetable oil

Kosher salt and freshly ground black pepper

1 medium onion, cut into $1/8$-inch dice (about 1 cup)

2 medium carrots, cut into $1/8$-inch dice (about 1 cup)

2 stalks celery, cut into $1/8$-inch dice (about 1 cup)

2 cloves garlic, minced (about 1 tablespoon)

$1/2$ cup chicken stock (page 131) or beef stock (page 135)

2 eggs

2 tablespoons Worcestershire sauce

1 teaspoon Dijon mustard

$1 1/2$ cups (3 ounces) freshly grated Parmesan cheese

$1/4$ cup (about $1/2$ ounce) dried porcini mushrooms, ground to crumbs in a food processor

$1/4$ cup fresh bread crumbs

1 pound ground chuck

1 pound extra-firm tofu, pressed and crumbled (see page 57)

$1/2$ cup ketchup

$1/4$ cup balsamic vinegar

1 teaspoon hot sauce

3 tablespoons brown sugar

TO COOK THE ONION MIXTURE, in a large, heavy-bottomed pan over medium-low heat, combine the bacon fat, oil, a pinch of salt, and the onion. Caramelize the onion slowly for about 30 minutes, stirring occasionally and reducing the heat if it browns too quickly. When the onion is completely soft and a deep brown, turn the heat up to medium-high, add the carrots, celery, and garlic, and sauté for about 1 minute. Add the stock and bring to a boil, stirring to scrape the browned bits from the bottom of the pan. Reduce the liquid by half. Set aside to cool slightly.

Preheat the oven to 375°F.

TO MIX AND FORM THE LOAF, in a large bowl, whisk the eggs, Worcestershire sauce, and mustard. Add the cheese, onion mixture, mushrooms, bread crumbs, beef, tofu, 2 teaspoons salt, and a few grinds of pepper. Mix gently to combine and form into a loaf on a rimmed baking sheet. Bake for 1 hour.

TO MAKE THE GLAZE, while the loaf is baking, combine the ketchup, vinegar, hot sauce, $1/2$ teaspoon salt, and the brown sugar in a saucepan over medium-high heat. Bring to a boil, reduce to a simmer, and cook for about 5 minutes, until it resembles syrup.

TO GLAZE AND SERVE, after the loaf has finished baking, remove from the oven, preheat the broiler, and brush the loaf with the glaze. Keeping a close watch on it, broil for 5 to 8 minutes, until the glaze has browned. Let the loaf cool for at least 20 minutes before slicing.

CARAMELIZED **ONIONS**

Caramelized onions are among the most delicious burger and steak toppings, but this technique will lend a balanced sweetness and depth of flavor to almost any savory dish. They are a welcome addition to sandwiches and casseroles. Caramelized onions can be finely chopped to a paste and mixed into salad dressing and soups or served alongside grilled meats or vegetables. Even at breakfast, these deeply browned onions make a fantastic addition to softly scrambled eggs.

To make them, you'll need two or more large onions, halved and cut into $1/8$-inch slices. Heat a 12-inch cast iron pan on low and add the sliced onions with enough olive oil to coat. Cook the onions for about 1 hour, or until they become meltingly soft and take on a rich brown color. Salt to taste and refrigerate for up to a week or freeze for three months.

Philly Cheesesteak

Three famous Philadelphia cheesesteak stands are situated on the journey between our two houses. On any given day, at nearly any hour, hungry people line up, lured by the beefy smells wafting off the flattop grill. We decided we'd be remiss to deliver this chapter void of a rendition of our city's signature sandwich. But doing so is also a risk, as Philadelphians take the meaty construction of cheesesteaks very seriously. With all due respect, we offer this version, which starts with paper-thin slices of rib eye roast (ask your butcher or look for packaged meat labeled "sandwich steaks" at the supermarket), skillet seared and smeared with cheese sauce. We add caramelized onions and malted portobellos for a treat so good it's worth waiting in line for. **Serves 4**

1 tablespoon all-purpose flour

$^1/_2$ cup milk

1 cup grated sharp cheddar cheese

6 portobello mushroom caps, sliced into $^1/_4$-inch strips

3 tablespoons malt vinegar

Kosher salt and freshly ground black pepper

1 tablespoon vegetable oil

1 medium yellow onion, sliced thin

8 ounces thin slices rib eye roast

$^1/_4$ cup water

4 steak rolls

TO MAKE THE CHEESE SAUCE, in a small saucepan, whisk together the flour and 1 tablespoon of the milk to form a smooth paste, free of lumps. Place the pan over medium heat and whisk in the remaining milk. Bring the mixture to a simmer and whisk for about 2 minutes, until it starts to thicken. Stir in the cheese until it melts into the milk, reduce the heat to low, and keep warm.

TO COOK THE MUSHROOMS AND ONIONS, toss the mushrooms with the vinegar. Season with salt and pepper and set aside. Heat the oil in a large skillet over medium heat. Add the onion and sauté for about 10 minutes, until it begins to soften and caramelize. Add the mushrooms and cook for an additional 5 minutes. Remove from the skillet, cover to keep warm, and set aside.

TO FRY THE STEAKS, return the skillet to the burner and increase the heat to medium-high. Fry the steak slices for about 30 seconds per side, or until cooked. Work in batches to avoid crowding the pan, adding the finished slices to the covered onion and mushrooms. When all the meat has been cooked and removed, add the water, and scrape the bottom to release the browned bits. Let simmer for about 30 seconds and then pour it over the reserved meat and vegetables.

TO ASSEMBLE THE SANDWICHES, distribute the steak evenly among the rolls and top with spoonfuls of mushrooms and onions. Season with salt and pepper and drizzle with cheese sauce (if the sauce has thickened, whisk in a splash of milk to loosen).

:tip: *On the East Coast you can definitely get meat labeled "sandwich steaks," but elsewhere, you might have to ask for rib eye roast, thinly sliced. Don't ask for rib eye steaks, thinly sliced— they're not the same thing.*

French Onion Soup

The perfect place to make the case for the impact of a homemade stock is from within a crock of dark, rich French onion soup. Slowly caramelized onions melt into an already heady beef stock, intense from roasted bones steeped with vegetables. A signature gratin of cheese atop a toasted baguette raft makes a serving surprisingly satiating. You can make this soup from store-bought broth, but the body of from-scratch beef stock is the secret ingredient that differentiates it from a one-dimensional bowl of onions and liquid. **Serves 4 to 6**

2 tablespoons butter

2 tablespoons olive oil

3 pounds yellow or white onions, sliced very thin (12 cups)

$1/2$ cup brandy

8 cups beef stock

2 large cloves garlic, smashed

2 sprigs thyme

1 bay leaf

2 tablespoons sherry vinegar

Salt and pepper

1 baguette, sliced into $1/2$-inch pieces and toasted

2 cups (8 ounces) grated Gruyère cheese

Melt the butter with the oil in a large Dutch oven over medium heat. Add the onions and cook slowly, stirring occasionally, for about 1 hour, until they sweat down and begin to turn deep golden. The onions will caramelize down to 2 cups.

Add half of the brandy, scraping the bits from the bottom of the pot. Add the rest of the brandy and simmer until nearly all of the liquid is gone. Add the stock, garlic, thyme, and bay leaf and simmer for 30 minutes.

Preheat the oven to 450°F.

Remove the bay leaf and stir in the vinegar. Season to taste with salt and pepper. Ladle the soup into bowls (one serving is about 1 cup), top each with 2 slices of bread, and $1/4$ cup cheese. Transfer the bowls to a rimmed baking sheet and then into the oven. Bake for about 10 minutes, until the cheese is bubbly and beginning to brown. Put the hot bowls on plates and serve.

Steak Salad with Blue Cheese Dressing

Unimaginative bowls of mixed greens have earned salads a bad reputation for being rabbit food. But peppery arugula fanned with a few thin slices of juicy, medium-rare steak, sprinkled with a flurry of nuts, a handful of apple slices, and a deceptively light but creamy blue cheese dressing turns a boring plate of greens into a supper to savor. **Serves 4**

12 ounces flank steak or skirt steak, at room temperature

1 teaspoon canola oil

Salt and freshly ground black pepper

4 ounces silken tofu, cut into cubes

3 ounces Maytag or other good-quality, flavorful blue cheese, crumbled (about $^3/_4$ cup)

2 tablespoons water

3 tablespoons buttermilk

1 teaspoon freshly squeezed lemon juice

1 tablespoon minced shallot

$^1/_4$ teaspoon Worcestershire sauce

1 large bunch arugula

$^1/_4$ cup pine nuts, toasted

1 crisp tart apple (such as Gala, Pink Lady, or Braeburn), halved, cored, and thinly sliced

Heat a grill pan or large sauté pan (not nonstick, preferably cast iron) over high heat, just until it begins to smoke. Drizzle the steak with the oil, and sprinkle with salt and pepper. Place the steak in the hot pan and let it sear for 4 minutes without moving it. Flip the steak with tongs and cook for another 2 to 4 minutes for medium-rare (about 130°F on a meat thermometer). Set aside to rest for at least 10 minutes and then, cutting across the grain, slice the steak into thin pieces.

Meanwhile, make the dressing by putting the tofu, cheese, water, buttermilk, lemon juice, shallot, Worcestershire sauce, $^1/_4$ teaspoon salt, and 5 grinds of pepper into a blender. Blend on high until a smooth creamy dressing has formed. Taste for seasoning and adjust as needed.

Divide the arugula over 4 plates. Scatter the pine nuts and apple slices evenly over the greens. Fan a few slices of steak over each serving and drizzle with blue cheese dressing.

tip: *When searing steak indoors on a grill pan or skillet, turn on your range hood or crack a window as it can get smoky.*

Chimichurri Fajitas

Fajitas are great for a crowd and the perfect recipe for incorporating small amounts of meat with lots of complementary ingredients. This version calls on *chimichurri* sauce, the staple condiment of Argentina, which is also home to the culinary world's best known grass-fed beef. If you are serving fewer people, cut the steak in half across the grain and tightly wrap and freeze the other half, or use it for Steak Salad with Blue Cheese Dressing (page 92). Make these fajitas all veggie by swapping in portobellos, bell peppers, and eggplant for the steak. Serve with rice, black beans, and salad. Flank steak and skirt steak are both good cuts for fajitas and are best cooked to medium-rare. **Serves 6 to 8**

Chimichurri

4 cups loosely packed fresh parsley leaves

2 cups loosely packed fresh cilantro leaves

1 medium jalapeño, seeded and coarsely chopped

3 cloves garlic

$1/2$ teaspoon toasted cumin seeds

1 teaspoon salt

$1/2$ teaspoon freshly ground black pepper

2 tablespoons freshly squeezed lime juice (about 2 limes)

2 tablespoons red wine vinegar

$1/2$ cup olive oil

Fajitas

1 medium green zucchini (about 1 pound), sliced $1/4$ inch thick lengthwise

1 medium yellow zucchini (about 1 pound), sliced $1/4$ inch thick lengthwise

Salt and pepper

1 medium red onion, sliced into $1/4$-inch-thick rings

1 flank steak or skirt steak (about $1^1/2$ pounds)

12 or more 6-inch flour or corn tortillas

1 cup sour cream (optional)

1 cup grated cheddar cheese (optional)

TO MAKE THE CHIMICHURRI, combine the parsley, cilantro, jalapeño, garlic, cumin seeds, salt, pepper, lime juice, and vinegar in the bowl of a food processor. Pulse three or four times, forming a coarse paste. With the processor running, add the oil through the food chute in a steady stream, forming a textured sauce. Taste for seasoning and adjust as needed. Reserve $1/4$ cup of the sauce for the marinade, and transfer the rest to a small serving bowl and set aside.

TO MAKE THE FAJITAS FIXINGS, lightly brush the zucchini strips with half of the reserved chimichurri, sprinkle with salt and pepper, and place in a zippered storage bag along with the onion. Season the steak with pepper and rub the remaining chimichurri on both sides. Let the zucchini and the steak sit at room temperature for 30 minutes.

Preheat the grill to medium-high.

Season the steak with salt and grill for 6 to 8 minutes per side for medium-rare. At the same time, grill the zucchini slices and onion rings for about 3 minutes per side, until grill marks appear and the vegetables are just tender. Transfer the grilled zucchini and onions to a plate, stacking them so the heat continues to cook them a bit. Grill the tortillas for about 30 seconds per side, until warm and slightly blackened. Wrap in foil to keep warm.

Remove the steak from the grill and let it sit for about 10 minutes. Slice the meat very thin, across the grain.

TO ASSEMBLE THE FAJITAS, pile 2 strips of steak and several pieces of zucchini and onion on each grilled tortilla. Drizzle with chimichurri sauce and roll it up, or leave the assembly to the crowd. Serve with sour cream and cheese if you like.

Butternut and Oxtail Stuffed Poblanos

Lumped in with "variety meats" like tongue and heart in old cookbooks, oxtail is really a cow's tail. It's among the least expensive cuts you'll find at the butcher. When braised for several hours, this afterthought of the beef world provides flavorful morsels for soups, stews, dumplings, and this stuffed pepper. This dish does take several hours, but the steps are very easy. And the resulting meal is the kind of Sunday supper that will fortify you for the week. If you are short on time, substitute cooked ground beef, chicken, turkey, pork, or even black beans for the oxtail. **Serves 4**

1 pound oxtail, medium to large cross-section pieces

Kosher salt and freshly ground black pepper

3 tablespoons olive oil

1/4 cup dry red wine

2 cloves garlic, smashed and peeled

1 bay leaf

2 cups beef stock (page 135)

1 small butternut squash, peeled and chopped into 1-inch cubes (about 2 cups)

1 medium russet potato

6 ounces soft fresh goat cheese

4 large poblano chiles, sliced in half lengthwise and seeded

Preheat the oven to 350°F. Space two racks so that a baking dish and a Dutch oven will fit.

TO PREPARE THE OXTAIL, season liberally with salt and pepper. Heat 1 tablespoon of the oil in a heavy-bottomed Dutch oven over medium-high heat. Brown the oxtail pieces on all sides, for about 2 minutes per side, for a total of about 8 minutes. Remove from the pot and set aside. Pour the wine into the empty pot and stir, picking up the browned bits, simmering for 3 to 5 minutes, until the wine has reduced by half. Return the oxtail pieces to the pot. Add the garlic, bay leaf, and enough of the beef stock to come halfway up the sides of the oxtail pieces. Cover the pot and then place it on the bottom rack in the preheated oven. Cook for 2 1/2 hours, turning occasionally and adding stock if needed to maintain the liquid level.

TO PREPARE THE SQUASH AND THE POTATO, when about 1 1/2 hours of cooking time remain for the oxtail, toss the squash with the remaining 2 tablespoons oil and season liberally with salt and pepper. Spread in a single layer on a rimmed baking sheet. Poke steam holes in the potato and place it, along with the squash, on the upper rack of the oven. Roast both for about 1 hour, or until they are tender when poked with a fork.

When cool enough to handle, split the potato in half and scrape the flesh with a spoon into the bowl of a stand mixer (or use a handheld mixer), discarding the skins. Add the roasted butternut squash and 4 ounces of the goat cheese and mix thoroughly with the paddle attachment. Season the mash with salt and pepper to taste and set aside.

TO ASSEMBLE THE DISH, when the meat is very tender and falling from the bones, transfer the oxtail to a plate and shred the meat. Meanwhile, strain the cooking liquid and let settle for 10 minutes (use a gravy separator if you have one). Skim the fat from the top, pour the defatted cooking liquid over the shredded oxtail, and set aside.

Arrange the poblano halves on a baking dish. Layer each with the oxtail pieces and cover with the butternut squash mixture, distributing evenly. Crumble the remaining 2 ounces goat cheese over the tops of the stuffed poblanos and bake for 30 minutes. Broil for a minute or two at the end to lightly brown the tops, if you like. Serve two poblano halves per person.

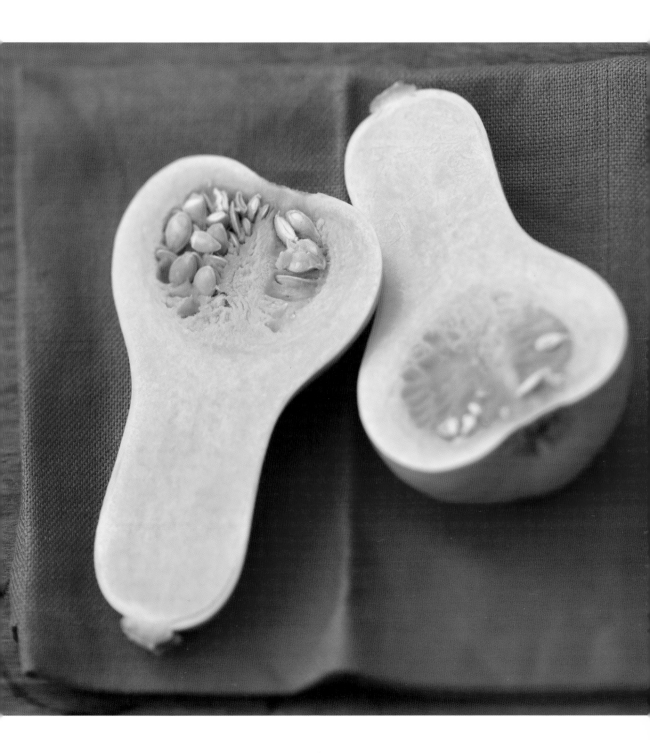

Spinach and Chickpea Pouches

This recipe bumps up tasty spanakopita triangles to meal-size pouches full of vegetables, chickpeas, creamy sharp feta cheese, and just a little bit of beef. They can be made vegetarian by simply omitting the meat. A Greek salad full of crunchy greens, cool cucumbers, and light lemony vinaigrette is the perfect accompaniment to make these rectangles a square meal. **Serves 6**

2 teaspoons vegetable oil

8 ounces ground beef

1 small red onion, sliced into thin strips

8 cups (about 6 ounces) loosely packed fresh spinach, coarsely chopped

1/4 teaspoon dried chile flakes

2 cloves garlic, minced (about 1 tablespoon)

1 tablespoon fresh oregano leaves, chopped

1 roasted red bell pepper, cut into thin strips (about 1 cup)

1 1/2 cups dried chickpeas, cooked, or 1 (15-ounce) can, drained and rinsed

Kosher salt and freshly ground black pepper

12 sheets filo dough, each lightly brushed with olive oil

1/2 cup feta cheese

1 egg, lightly beaten

1 tablespoon lightly toasted sesame seeds

1/2 cup tzatziki (page 111), plain Greek yogurt, or sour cream

Preheat the oven to 375°F.

TO MAKE THE FILLING, heat the oil in a sauté pan over medium-high heat. Crumble in the ground beef and cook, stirring occasionally to break up the pieces. When the meat is cooked through, remove it from the pan and set aside. Add the onion, spinach, chile flakes, garlic, and oregano to the pan and sauté until the spinach wilts. Remove from the heat and stir in the cooked beef, pepper strips, and chickpeas. Season the mixture with salt and pepper.

TO ASSEMBLE AND BAKE, cut the 12 sheets of filo dough in half horizontally so you have 24 rectangles. Stash the filo you are not working with under a damp tea towel to prevent drying. Divide into 6 stacks of 4. Place 1/2 cup of the beef mixture in a long mound toward the center of each stack, sprinkle with 1 heaping tablespoon of the feta cheese, and fold up the sides to enclose. Transfer each pouch, seam side down, to a rimmed baking sheet lined with a silicone mat or parchment paper. Brush the tops of each pouch with the egg and sprinkle with sesame seeds. Transfer to the oven and bake for 15 to 20 minutes, until the dough is golden brown.

Serve each pouch with a dollop of tzatziki.

Shabu-Shabu Soup

Shabu-shabu is a popular Japanese dish that consists of a sizable platter of paper-thin slices of raw beef, another large plate of raw vegetables, and a big pot of simmering broth. Each diner dips his or her own ingredients in the broth, which cooks the meat and vegetables quickly. It takes its name from the description of the sound the ingredients make when swishing through the broth. In our version, all the ingredients are cooked ahead and doled out into bowls. Serve with chopsticks for fetching the meat, vegetables, and noodles, plus a spoon for slurping the delicious broth.

Serves 4 to 6

2 teaspoons vegetable oil

1 bok choy, thinly sliced (about 4 cups)

1 medium carrot, peeled into strips lengthwise

4 scallions, white and green parts, thinly sliced

1 cup (about 4 ounces) sliced shiitake mushrooms

8 cups mushroom broth (page 138)

2 tablespoons soy sauce, divided

3 ounces soba noodles

4 ounces paper-thin slices rib eye roast, cut into $1/2$-inch strips

$1/4$ teaspoon dark (Asian) sesame oil

1 tablespoon rice wine vinegar

Salt and freshly ground black pepper

Heat the oil in a Dutch oven or stockpot over medium-high heat. Add the bok choy, carrot, white parts of the scallions, and mushrooms and sauté for about 2 minutes, just until the bok choy greens begin to wilt. Add the stock and 1 tablespoon of the soy sauce, lower the heat to medium, and simmer for 10 minutes. Add the soba noodles, simmering for an additional 5 minutes. Bring the liquid to a boil and drop in the strips of beef. Cook for 30 seconds, drop the heat to low, stir in the remaining 1 tablespoon soy sauce, sesame oil, and vinegar, and season to taste with salt and pepper. Remove from the heat and ladle the soup into bowls, using tongs to grab vegetables, noodles, and meat. Sprinkle the green parts of the scallions on top of the soup and serve.

> **tip:** *It's important that the slices of beef are paper-thin so they cook quickly. If "steak sandwich" slices aren't already available packaged in the supermarket cases, ask the meat department for thinly sliced rib eye. Your butcher shop will likely do this to order anyway.*

Light on Lamb

*Demand for lamb may pale in comparison to beef and pork,
but this flavorful meat has many hidden virtues.*

In the 1940s, Americans ate an average of 6 pounds of lamb per year. Lamb never made up a majority of the meat market, but at that rate most Americans were familiar enough with its savory personality. During the intervening decades, lamb has become less and less common on our tables. The decline started when tastes changed as soldiers trickled back to the States after World War II. During their overseas deployments, many ate mutton, an often ill-prepared and unpleasant meat from a much older sheep. Lamb acquired a reputation for tasting gamey and sour, qualities you might find in mutton, but not a well-prepared lamb, which is always less than a year old. Today, sadly, we eat less than 1 pound of lamb each year. According to the American Lamb Board, only one in five Americans has prepared lamb in the last year.

The loss of the American meat popularity contest has an upside. With substantially less demand, it becomes more viable for small farms to raise lamb as nature intended, as grass-fed ruminants. Both kinds of lamb available to U.S. consumers, domestic and New Zealand, are often grass fed. Some U.S. ranchers finish their lambs on grain at feed lots to produce the fattier, mild taste and tender texture Americans love, but the vast majority of New Zealand lamb is pastured throughout its life. Domestic lamb, of course, doesn't require a plane ride to get to your table. If, like most Americans, you haven't cooked much with lamb, you should sample both varieties and choose according to your taste. It's best to find organic lamb that's raised on small-scale farms, free from antibiotics, hormones, and other chemicals.

Lamb's best virtue, though, might be its nutrition profile. The tender meat is high in zinc, a key mineral for good immune function and healing, and selenium, a trace element that helps prevent cell damage.

LAMB PARTS

When most of us think of lamb, we envision a regal roasted rack, each slender bone crowned in little white toques. But we urge you to consider recipes in which lamb shares the spotlight with other ingredients. Cuts of lamb are often available in small amounts, but if you buy more than you need, just wrap the remainder tightly, freeze, and use within a few months.

Leg: Often boned, butterflied, stuffed, and rolled before being grilled or roasted. Ask your butcher to cut you a smaller portion or a "leg steak" to marinate, grill, and slice thin for salads and sandwiches like Ful Mudammas Gyros (page 111). Cubed leg meat is good for kebabs.

Shanks: Cut from the lower forelegs and sometimes the hind legs, these are the perfect choice for braising. Restaurants typically serve a whole shank per person, but the same amount makes a rich shepherd's pie (page 106) to feed a family.

Whole shoulder: This is an impressive piece of meat for roasting and serving as the centerpiece of a meat-centric meal. Smaller cuts of it, like the round chops and the blade chops, are perfect for infusing a ton of flavor and just the

right amount of meat into a ragu like the one paired with our almond gnocchi (page 105).

Neck: These pieces are a good alternative to stew meat or shoulder chops for braising. Often available bone in, the collagen adds body to sauces and stews. Just cut the meat away from the bones after a long braise.

Loin: This meat is good for grilling or broiling and is available in smaller pieces.

Stew meat: This is usually cubed boneless shoulder meat for braising and stewing.

Ground lamb: A combo of trimmings from all of the cuts, it's the obvious choice for burgers. It is also excellent for lending big lamb flavor with just a small quantity as in Stuffed Grape Leaves (page 110) and Spiced Lamb and Vegetable Stew (page 109).

Almond Gnocchi with Lamb Ragu

Gnocchi are another member of the pasta family with an intimidating reputation. They can be heavy with starch instead of perfectly pillow-y. But ours are soft, tender, and light with a touch of texture from almond flour. Ricing the potatoes prevents them from getting sticky and glutinous. We recommend boiling three small potatoes, rather than one large one, because it will take less time. Just a couple of shoulder chops offer meaty lamb flavor to a hearty, rustic ragu that can be as delicious without the meat (just pick up the recipe with the onions and garlic and simmer for 30 minutes). **Serves 4**

Gnocchi

3 small russet potatoes (about 1 pound), unpeeled and scrubbed

$3/4$ cup all-purpose flour

$1/2$ cup almond flour

$1/4$ cup freshly grated Parmesan cheese (1 ounce), plus more for serving

Kosher salt and freshly ground black pepper

1 egg yolk

Lamb Ragu

$1/2$ pound lamb shoulder round chops

Kosher salt and freshly ground black pepper

1 tablespoon olive oil

1 cup small-diced onion

2 large cloves garlic, sliced very thin

$1/2$ cup red wine

1 (28-ounce) can whole peeled tomatoes, seeded and crushed

3 fresh sage leaves

1 sprig oregano

TO PREPARE THE POTATOES FOR THE GNOCCHI, put the unpeeled potatoes in a large pot and fill it with cold water. Bring the water to a boil, then simmer the potatoes for 30 minutes, or until fork tender all the way through. Turn off the heat, remove the potatoes from the water with a slotted spoon, and run cold water over them. Set them aside to cool slightly. Reserve the hot water in the pot.

TO MAKE THE RAGU, season the lamb with salt and pepper. Heat the oil in a large sauté pan over high heat. Add the lamb to the pan and sear the pieces for about 5 minutes on each side, until nicely browned. Remove the lamb from the pan and set aside. Add the onion and garlic and sauté for 2 minutes. Pour in the wine, scraping the browned bits from the bottom of the pan. Add the tomatoes, sage, and oregano. Reduce the heat to medium low, cover the pan, and braise the lamb in the sauce for $1^1/2$ hours.

TO MAKE THE GNOCCHI, while the lamb cooks, whisk together the flours, cheese, and 1 table-spoon salt in a large bowl. Peel the potatoes, discarding the skins, and squeeze them through a ricer into the flour mixture. Add the egg yolk and gently stir all the ingredients together, forming a soft dough. If the dough is too sticky, add flour a few teaspoons at a time, taking care not to add too much. Knead the dough about 10 times and then cut it into 8 smaller pieces. Roll each piece

continued . . .

into a $^1/_2$-inch-thick rope, and cut into $^1/_2$-inch pieces. Transfer the pieces to a rimmed baking sheet dusted with flour. Return the pot of water to a boil and season with salt.

TO FINISH THE DISH, when the meat is very tender, take the chops out of the sauce. Shred the meat with two forks and return it to the pan, discarding the bones. Remove the sage leaves and the oregano sprig, season with salt and pepper to taste, and keep the ragu warm.

Gently drop batches of the gnocchi into the boiling water and cook for about 3 minutes, until the gnocchi float to the top of the pot. Transfer the cooked gnocchi with a slotted spoon into the warm ragu. Continue until all of the gnocchi are cooked.

Gently toss the gnocchi with the ragu over low heat. Divide the gnocchi and lamb ragu into serving bowls, sprinkle with cheese, and serve.

Shepherd's Pie

Most Americans are introduced to this casserole in Irish bars where it is often served as bland and flavorless cubes of beef topped with gluey instant mashed potatoes. Our flavorful version is hearty, filling, and still a perfect partner for a pint. Plus, it has its roots in the dish's real history; shepherds in Ireland were more likely to use lamb than beef. We also opt to braise a lamb shank and use the moist, tender meat and its sauce as a base for the chock-full-of-vegetables stew. The potato topping is true to tradition and as simple as it gets. **Serves 4 to 6**

1 (1-pound) lamb shank

Kosher salt and freshly ground black
    pepper

1 tablespoon olive oil

2 large shallots, sliced into $^1/_8$-inch rings

1 small onion, cut into $^1/_2$-inch dice (about
    1 cup)

3 cloves garlic, coarsely chopped

$1^1/_2$ cups dry red wine

2 medium carrots, cut into $^1/_2$-inch dice
    (about 1 cup)

1 cup frozen lima beans

$1^3/_4$ cups beef stock (page 135)

1 sprig thyme

1 bay leaf

3 large russet potatoes (2 pounds total)

$^1/_4$ cup sour cream

$^1/_2$ cup whole milk

Preheat the oven to 400°F.

TO PREPARE THE STEW, season the lamb shank with salt and pepper. Heat the oil in a Dutch oven over medium-high heat. Add the lamb shank, browning on all sides, for a total of about 10 minutes. Remove the shank and set aside.

Add the shallots, onion, and garlic to the pot and sauté for 5 minutes. Add $^1/_2$ cup of the wine and simmer until most of the liquid is gone. Stir in the carrots and lima beans and then return the shank to the pot. Add the remaining 1 cup wine and the stock along with the thyme and bay leaf. Cover the pot, tilting the lid up just a crack, and transfer to the middle rack in the oven for $1^1/_2$ hours.

TO PREPARE THE POTATOES, poke steam holes all over each potato and bake for 1 hour in the same oven while the lamb braises. After 1 hour, remove the potatoes from the oven and let cool for about 10 minutes. Cut each in half and scoop out the insides to a bowl. Add the sour cream and milk and season to taste with salt and pepper. Mash the potatoes by hand, or use a mixer for a smoother consistency. Set aside.

TO FINISH THE STEW, remove the pot from the oven and transfer the shank to a plate. When cool enough to handle, shred the meat from the bone with two forks. Return the meat to the sauce and vegetables in the pot, and stir to combine all of the ingredients. Taste for seasoning and adjust as needed.

TO ASSEMBLE THE PIE, pour the lamb and vegetable mixture into a 9-inch deep-dish pie plate. Spread the mashed potatoes over the top. Bake the pie for 20 minutes, or until the top begins to turn golden brown. Let the pie sit for 5 minutes and then scoop servings onto plates or wide shallow bowls.

> **tip** *Potato skins are full of good flavor and are perfect for sopping up the thick, hearty sauce from the stew of this pie. After scraping the potato from the skins, put them on a rimmed baking sheet alongside the pie for the last 20 minutes in the oven. Serve pieces of the crispy skins underneath a helping of the stew or on the side for mopping up what's left on the plate when you're through.*

Spiced Lamb and Vegetable Stew

Indian cuisine's appeal comes from characteristic spice blends that can often be hard to find. This dish draws on some of our favorite Indian flavors but keeps your shopping trip simple with no obscure ingredients. In Indian cuisine, lamb appears where the American palate would expect beef. That's because in this mostly Hindu country, cows are revered as sacred animals. (There, lamb is the stuff Big Macs are made of—in an Indian McDonald's you can order a lamb burger, but not a hamburger.) We pair the meat with plenty of potato and aromatic spices like garam masala, coriander, and cumin. Creating a vegetarian version of this flavorful stew is as simple as omitting the lamb. Ladle the stew over basmati rice and serve with warm naan. **Serves 4 to 6 (makes 4 cups of stew)**

1 teaspoon vegetable oil

$1/2$ teaspoon cumin seeds

$1/4$ pound ground lamb

2 tablespoons minced fresh ginger

3 cloves garlic, minced (about 2 tablespoons)

1 small onion, cut into $1/4$-inch dice (about 1 cup)

2 medium carrots, cut into $1/4$-inch dice (about 1 cup)

2 Yukon gold potatoes, cut into $1/4$-inch dice (about $1^1/2$ cups)

1 medium tomato, diced (about 1 cup)

2 dried chiles de árbol, rehydrated, seeded, and chopped

$1/2$ cup water

$1/2$ cup tomato puree

$1/2$ teaspoon turmeric

1 teaspoon ground coriander

2 cups loosely packed chopped fresh spinach

$1^1/2$ teaspoons salt

Freshly ground black pepper

1 teaspoon garam masala

Heat the vegetable oil in a Dutch oven or large pot over medium heat. Add the cumin seeds and sauté for about 30 seconds, just until fragrant. Add the lamb and cook, stirring frequently to break up the meat, for about 5 minutes, until brown. Stir in the ginger, garlic, and onion, sautéing for 5 minutes more. Add the carrots, potatoes, tomato, chiles, water, tomato puree, turmeric, coriander, and spinach, mixing to incorporate all of the ingredients.

Reduce the heat to low, cover, and simmer, stirring occasionally, for about 45 minutes, or until the potatoes and carrots are tender.

Add salt and pepper to taste, and garam masala. Mix well to combine the seasonings, taste and adjust as necessary, and serve.

Stuffed Grape Leaves

A mainstay of Greek restaurants, stuffed grape leaves can be prepared a million different ways. Some are vegetarian, others have meat. Some are served hot and others are chilled. Some are bright and lemony while others have earthy undertones. This mostly vegetarian version does incorporate a bit of ground lamb, but it could easily be omitted with no adverse effects. Stuffed grape leaves are typically served as a snack or appetizer, but with some good flatbread, hummus, and feta, they can take center stage in a meal of mezes. **Makes 30**

1 cup water

$1/2$ cup long-grain white rice

1 tablespoon olive oil

$1/4$ pound ground lamb

$1/2$ cup minced onion

2 cloves garlic, pressed

$1/4$ teaspoon cinnamon

$1/4$ cup pine nuts, toasted

2 tablespoons chopped fresh parsley

Salt and pepper

1 (16 ounce) jar grape leaves, rinsed and dried, stems trimmed (30 leaves)

1 lemon, cut into wedges

1 cup Greek yogurt

TO MAKE THE FILLING, bring the water to a boil, add the rice, cover, and reduce the heat to low. Cook for 20 minutes, then remove from the heat, keeping covered, and set aside.

Heat the oil over medium-high heat in a large sauté pan. Add the lamb and cook for 8 to 10 minutes, until brown. Scoop the meat from the pan and set aside on a plate. Add the onion and garlic to the same pan and sauté for 5 minutes, until softened but not browning. Return the lamb to the pan and add the cinnamon. Sauté the mixture for another 2 minutes, then remove from the heat and transfer to a large bowl. Stir in the cooked rice, pine nuts, and parsley. Season to taste with salt and pepper.

TO ASSEMBLE AND SERVE, preheat the oven to 350°F. Arrange the grape leaves on a clean work surface, smooth side down. Place a tablespoon of filling in the center of each leaf. Pull the top and bottom of the leaf over the filling and then roll from one side to the other to wrap the filling like a burrito. Place each stuffed leaf seam side down on a rimmed baking sheet. Transfer to the oven to heat through, for about 10 minutes.

Serve on a large platter with lemon wedges and yogurt.

Ful Mudammas Gyros

Gyros are the famous Mediterranean street sandwiches known for the lamb shaved from a giant column of rotating roasted meat. In our version, marinated leg of lamb is grilled and sliced thin, then tucked into super-soft pita bread with hearty bean spread and cool, creamy *tzatziki*. If you can't find canned fava beans to make a quick version of the thick garlicky *ful mudammas* bean spread, use a combination of cooked white beans and chickpeas. **Serves 4**

Tzatziki
1/2 cucumber, cut into 1/4-inch dice (about 1/2 cup)

1/2 cup Greek yogurt

1 clove garlic, minced and mashed to a paste with 1/4 teaspoon kosher salt

1/4 cup loosely packed fresh mint leaves, chopped (optional)

Salt (optional)

Lamb
1 (12-ounce) leg of lamb steak

Zest of 1/2 lemon

1 tablespoon freshly squeezed lemon juice

2 tablespoons olive oil

2 teaspoons chopped fresh oregano leaves

2 cloves garlic, minced or crushed

1/4 teaspoon freshly ground black pepper

Ful Mudammas
1 1/2 cups fava beans, cooked, or 1 (15-ounce) can, drained and rinsed

1 clove garlic, minced and mashed to a paste with 1/4 teaspoon kosher salt

Zest of 1/2 lemon

Juice of 1/2 lemon (about 2 tablespoons)

1 tablespoon olive oil

1/2 cup loosely packed fresh parsley leaves, chopped

Kosher salt and freshly ground black pepper

4 pocketless pitas or flatbreads

2 pounds tomatoes, chopped

TO MAKE THE TZATZIKI, combine the cucumber, yogurt, garlic, and mint if desired in a small bowl and stir until combined. Taste, adding salt if needed. Cover and refrigerate until you're ready to use.

TO MARINATE THE LAMB, whisk together the lemon zest, lemon juice, olive oil, oregano, garlic, and pepper in a large glass bowl. Add the lamb and flip the meat several times to coat in the marinade. Cover the bowl and refrigerate for 1 hour.

TO MAKE THE FUL MUDAMMAS, while the lamb marinates, combine the beans, garlic, lemon zest, lemon juice, olive oil, parsley, and salt and pepper to taste. Smash the beans with a pestle, fork, or a wooden spoon to form a textured paste. Season with additional salt if necessary.

Preheat the grill to medium-high. Place the lamb on the hot grill and discard the remaining marinade. Grill for about 4 minutes per side, until the meat reaches medium-rare (about 130°F on a meat thermometer). Take the lamb off the grill and let it rest for about 5 minutes before slicing very thinly across the grain.

TO ASSEMBLE, put about 1/4 cup of the fava bean mixture on each pita or flatbread. Add 3 or 4 slices of lamb, a spoonful of the chopped tomato, and a dollop of tzatziki, and wrap the pita around the filling. Repeat with the remaining ingredients, and serve.

Albóndigas

Albóndigas, the Spanish word for meatballs, is the proper name for this recipe even though it calls for only a half pound of meat. Steel-cut oats (also called Scotch or Irish oats) are oat groats that have not been rolled. Here, they serve as a chewy substitution for additional meat and soak up the flavors of spicy chipotle and the sauce. We recommend chunky-style crushed canned tomatoes, if you can find them. Serve the *albóndigas* in their sauce over lime rice and along with flour tortillas.

Serves 4 to 6

$1/2$ cup steel-cut oatmeal

$1/2$ cup loosely packed fresh cilantro leaves, chopped, plus more for garnish

4 cloves garlic, minced (about 2 tablespoons), divided

1 chipotle in adobo sauce, seeded and chopped into a paste

4 teaspoons ground cumin, divided

2 teaspoons ground coriander, divided

Kosher salt and freshly ground black pepper

$1/2$ pound ground lamb

2 teaspoons olive oil

1 small onion, cut into $1/4$-inch dice (about 1 cup)

1 (28-ounce) can crushed tomatoes

1 cup water

Juice of 1 lime

Mix together the oatmeal, cilantro, half the garlic, the chipotle, 2 teaspoons of the cumin, 1 teaspoon of the coriander, 1 teaspoon salt, and $1/4$ teaspoon pepper in a bowl. Gently work the lamb into the mixture, distributing it evenly. Form balls out of tablespoon-size scoops of the mixture and set aside.

Heat the oil in a Dutch oven or a large pot over medium-high heat. Add the onion and sauté for 5 minutes. Stir in the remaining garlic, cumin, and coriander, cooking for an additional 30 seconds. Add the tomatoes and water and stir to combine. Bring the sauce to a simmer and add the meatballs. Simmer partially covered for 45 minutes. Season the sauce with salt and pepper to taste, squeeze the lime juice over top, and serve with extra chopped cilantro.

Just Enough Eggs

Not just a breakfast staple, eggs can be enjoyed throughout the day in unexpected and simple meals.

Breakfast dishes are an obvious place for eggs, but few people realize their potential for taking center stage at dinner. Eggs emulsify sauces and add structure to baked goods, but they also stand on their own as a delicious centerpiece of a meal. They cook up more easily than most other protein sources and are certainly more economical. On those nights when you're so tired or pressed for time that cooking seems out of the question, consider our Grecian Frittata (page 123). Lyonnaise Salad (page 70) is also a fast and satisfying dish. Eggs make a whole range of elegant meals possible. It's the magic of a soufflé that makes our roulade (page 122) a showstopper perfect for company.

But not all eggs offer the same package of wholesome goodness. We seek out eggs laid by pastured hens within 50 miles of where we live. What is so special about them? Well, their freshness can't be surpassed. When you crack open these liquid jewels, you'll notice a yolk as yellow as sunshine. Unlike supermarket eggs, these beauties have a white that actually stands up and holds its shape. But differences aren't just aesthetic. Cooked over low heat to a soft scramble, these eggs have flavor that you just don't get from conventional hens. The taste is richer and far more complex. That's because pastured hens eat grass, bugs, and even flowers. Pecking around an old-fashioned barnyard lets them enjoy their natural diet and open-air way of life. And if the flavor and freshness benefits aren't compelling enough, remember: these eggs have 20 times more omega-3s, 10 percent less fat, 40 percent more vitamin A, and a whopping 34 percent less cholesterol than conventionally produced eggs.

Rich in nutrients, eggs provide a complete protein because they contain all nine essential amino acids. They're also rich in choline, which promotes brain health; lutein, which can help prevent heart disease; and folate, which helps promote new red blood cells. A large egg has only 75 calories, making it a good bargain for those who want to make every calorie count. Of course eggs also contain fat, 5 grams each, and up to 212 milligrams cholesterol. Increasingly, it is believed that saturated fat (an egg has only 1 gram) is a bigger culprit in heart disease than the cholesterol in food. Today's research is clear: the benefits of eating eggs as part of a nourishing diet far outweigh any possible cholesterol-rated risks. Some studies have actually shown participants' cholesterol going down on a diet rich in eggs, probably because eggs make such a sustaining breakfast. Those who start their days with a small vegetable-packed omelet are much less likely to snack on high-fat foods.

RAW **EGGS**

Some people are so worried about eating raw eggs that they never taste a cake batter before it goes into the oven. They don't know the joy of swabbing up egg yolks with a buttery piece of toast. They can't permit themselves one molecule of a heavenly homemade mayo. It is estimated that 1 in 20,000 eggs is contaminated with salmonella. You are more likely to get in a car wreck or become the victim of a violent crime than you are to get sick from a bad egg. Really. And farm-fresh eggs, usually cleaned and handled with more care than their factory counterparts, probably pose even less hazard. If you are still freaked out, you can always opt for pasteurized eggs, which are heated in their shells to kill off bacteria.

Stracciatella

Stracciatella is Italy's egg drop soup. The word *stracciatella* means little rags or little shreds and is given to the soup for the way the cooked eggs look in the broth. It couldn't be simpler to make and would pair well with our Croccante Signore (page 65) for an Italian-influenced soup and grilled cheese sandwich supper. Use rich homemade chicken stock or switch to vegetable or mushroom broth for a vegetarian version. **Serves 4**

4 cups chicken stock (page 131)

3 eggs

¼ teaspoon freshly grated nutmeg

½ cup freshly grated Parmesan cheese (2 ounces)

1 teaspoon kosher salt

Freshly ground black pepper

Juice of ½ lemon (about 2 tablespoons)

½ cup loosely packed fresh parsley leaves, chopped

Bring the stock to a boil in a large pot over medium-high heat. Whisk together the eggs, nutmeg, cheese, salt, and a few grinds of pepper in a bowl. Pour the egg mixture into the soup, stir twice, and then drop the heat to low. The eggs will set up and form strands throughout the liquid. Stir in the lemon juice and parsley, then adjust the seasoning to taste and ladle into bowls.

ADD AN **EGG**

We know it sounds crazy, but a lot of everyday foods taste better with a fried, poached, or hard-boiled egg tossed on top.

Burgers: Most burgers taste better with the addition of a fried egg.

Chili: Chili, especially our Beefed-Up Bean Chili (page 85), becomes a satisfying meal with a poached egg added just before serving.

Pizza: Some pizzerias even bake an egg right in the middle of their pies.

Leftovers: Various leftovers can be enhanced with an egg, especially rice, hash browns, or other potato side dishes. Fried or poached eggs work best.

Salads: Some cry out for a runny poached egg while others are right for a chopped hard-boiled egg, but most salads can use the protein boost.

Bean dishes: Simply cooked black beans or refried beans and rice make a nice bed for a fried egg.

Roasted vegetables: Again, runny yolks from a sunny side up egg transform a side dish into a saucy meal.

Springtime Spaghetti Carbonara

This pasta dish is known for its simple sauce that comes together quickly when whipped eggs meet the hot pasta. Carbonara is often grouped into the naughty foods category because the basic components of the recipe include cream, eggs, bacon, and cheese. But our recipe uses a dash of milk, just enough bacon for a hint of smoky flavor and crunch, and lots of fresh, vibrant peas, asparagus, and basil. Timing is the key to the creamy sauce; be sure all of the ingredients are ready to combine with the pasta as soon as it is al dente. Toss the spaghetti constantly in the eggs and cheese mixture for about 30 seconds to coat the pasta and prevent the eggs from scrambling.

Serves 4 to 6

3 slices bacon, cut into 1/4-inch pieces

1/2 pound English peas, shelled (about 1 cup), or 1/2 cup frozen peas

1 pound spaghetti

4 ounces asparagus, sliced diagonally 1/8 inch thick (1 cup)

10 fresh basil leaves, sliced thin

5 eggs, whisked, at room temperature

2 tablespoons whole milk

1/2 cup freshly grated Parmesan cheese, plus extra for garnish (2 ounces)

Kosher salt and freshly ground black pepper

Heat a sauté pan over medium heat and add the bacon, cooking for about 5 minutes, until crispy. Transfer the cooked bacon with a slotted spoon to a paper towel and set aside. Return the pan with the rendered fat to the stovetop for future use.

Bring a pot of salted water to a boil. Drop the peas into the water and cook them for 5 minutes. Transfer them to a strainer with a slotted spoon or a spider basket. Add the pasta to the boiling water and cook for 10 minutes, or until al dente.

While the pasta cooks, heat the bacon fat in the sauté pan over medium heat. Add the peas and asparagus, and sauté for about 5 minutes. Remove from the heat, stir in the basil, and set aside.

Whisk together the eggs and milk. Have the egg mixture, vegetables, and bacon ready to toss with very hot pasta.

Quickly drain the pasta and transfer immediately to a large serving bowl. Pour the eggs and cheese on top of the pasta, and toss vigorously to coat the strands and gently cook the eggs, forming a creamy sauce. Add the vegetables, and bacon, and continue tossing to incorporate them. Season with salt and pepper to taste.

Portion the spaghetti on plates and ladle any sauce left in the bowl over each serving. Grate additional cheese on top if you like.

Deviled Eggs

There's something deliciously retro about this classic party food, but you don't need a special occasion to whip up a batch. These make a terrific starter to any dinner, and they are especially good at rounding out a soup-and-salad supper or with anything coming off the grill. We call for a hefty dose of hot sauce because we like ours extra devilish. Feel free to cut back. And while the panko crumbs are optional, they add a pleasant textural contrast that many recipes lack.

Serves 4 to 8

1/4 cup (1/2 ounce) panko bread crumbs (optional)

1 dozen eggs, hard-boiled and peeled (see sidebar below)

2 teaspoons Dijon mustard

1/3 cup mayonnaise, prepared or homemade (page 17)

1/4 teaspoon turmeric

1 tablespoon grated shallot

1/2 teaspoon sriracha or other hot sauce

5 cornichons, diced

Salt and freshly ground black pepper

1 tablespoon sweet paprika for garnish

Preheat the oven to 350°F. Spread the panko crumbs on a rimmed baking sheet and bake for about 10 minutes, until slightly browned and crunchy. Set aside to cool.

Slice the eggs in half, scraping the yolks into a large bowl. Add the mustard, mayonnaise, turmeric, shallot, *sriracha*, and cornichons. Whisk until the mixture is smooth and creamy. Season to taste with salt and pepper.

Using a teaspoon, fill each egg half with a heaping teaspoon of the yolk mixture. (If you want to be fancy, you could use a piping bag to fill the eggs, but it isn't necessary.) Just before serving, top each yellow center with a heavy pinch of toasted panko crumbs and dust evenly with paprika.

HARD-BOILING EGGS

For perfect hard-boiled eggs: Fill a saucepan (large enough to hold all the eggs you are cooking in one layer) with cold water and add the eggs. Place the pan over medium-high heat. The moment the water comes to a boil, turn off the water, cover the pan, and let the eggs sit for 15 minutes for a fully cooked yolk. If you like your yolks set but not cooked firm, let the eggs sit for a few minutes less.

Transfer the cooked eggs with a slotted spoon from the hot water to a large bowl of cold water. When the eggs are cool enough to handle, tap each one gently to crack the shell a bit and return it to the cold water to cool completely, at least 15 minutes. Once cool, peel the shell from each egg and rinse it under cold water to remove any remaining bits of shell.

Oeufs en Meurette

This dish isn't widely made here in America, but it's a mainstay of France's many cafés. Though poached eggs are at the center of the dish, *oeufs en meurette* are much more dinner than breakfast thanks to the savory sauce made of beef stock and wine. In many cases, boxed beef stock works well in recipes, but this is one dish where a flavorful homemade stock makes a noticeable difference. And don't substitute a low-quality "cooking" wine for vino you'd want to drink. An inexpensive dry French table wine is perfect in the recipe and alongside this Parisian café classic.

Serves 4

2 tablespoons butter, divided	1 tablespoon red wine vinegar
2 slices bacon, diced	1 tablespoon white wine vinegar
1 small onion, cut into $\frac{1}{8}$-inch dice	8 eggs
$2\frac{1}{2}$ cups dry red wine	8 thick slices brioche, cut into rounds, toasted, and lightly buttered
$1\frac{1}{2}$ cups beef stock (page 135)	2 tablespoons chopped fresh parsley
2 sprigs thyme	
1 clove garlic, peeled and smashed	

Melt 1 tablespoon of the butter in a saucepan over medium heat. Add the bacon and cook for about 5 minutes, or until the pieces are crispy. Remove the pan from the heat and lift the bacon bits out with a slotted spoon, transferring them to a paper towel–lined plate.

Return the pan to medium-low heat. Add the onion and cook for about 10 minutes, until softened. Add the wine, stock, thyme, and garlic. Increase the heat to medium-high and bring to a simmer. Cook the liquid for 20 minutes, or until it has reduced to about 1 cup. Strain the liquid, discarding the solids, and return it to a saucepan over low heat to keep warm while you poach the eggs and make the toast rounds.

Fill a 10-inch, straight-sided pan with $1\frac{1}{2}$ inches of water (or use a Dutch oven or other large sauce pot). Add the vinegars and bring the liquid to a bare simmer, so that there are active bubbles, but the water is not rolling. Gently crack the eggs one by one, slipping them into the water and taking care not to break the yolks (you may need to do this in batches, depending on the size of your pan). Run a spoon through the water to prevent the eggs from sticking to the bottom. Reduce the heat to low and let the eggs cook for 3 to 5 minutes, or until the whites have set and the yolk is done to the desired consistency, and remove with a slotted spoon. Blot the bottom of the spoon on a kitchen towel to catch the draining water.

Arrange 2 toast rounds each on 4 warmed plates. Top each round with a poached egg, 2 tablespoons wine sauce, and a sprinkle of parsley.

Grits Roulade

A roulade is the soufflé's less-exacting sibling. It is similarly constructed, beginning with a thick base fortified with egg yolks, lightened with whipped egg whites, and ending with a bake in the oven that yields puffy results. A roulade's flat design, though, makes it more resilient than a soufflé. It can be baked in advance and served warm or at room temperature. Our version calls on hearty, unpretentious grits for the base and rolls in sweet honey ham and smoky Gouda for the flavors of a down-home country breakfast that can be served anytime. **Serves 4 to 6**

2 cups whole milk	Salt and freshly ground black pepper
$^1/_2$ cup grits (not instant)	5 eggs, separated
$^1/_4$ cup minced scallions, white and green parts	4 ounces thinly sliced honey ham
1 cup plus $^1/_4$ cup grated smoked Gouda or smoked cheddar cheese	

Preheat the oven to 350°F. Line a 10 by 15-inch rimmed baking sheet with parchment paper and lightly butter. Cut and butter another 10 by 15-inch piece of parchment paper and set aside.

TO PREPARE THE GRITS, in a pot over medium heat, bring the milk to a boil. Whisk in the grits and then reduce the heat slightly to prevent the milk from boiling over. Cook the grits for about 15 minutes, stirring regularly with a wooden spoon. Remove the grits from the heat and stir in the scallions, the $^1/_4$ cup cheese, and 2 teaspoons salt. Taste and add salt and pepper as needed.

TO MAKE THE ROULADE BATTER, whisk the egg yolks together in a large bowl. Add about $^1/_4$ cup of the hot grits to the yolks and whisk together quickly to raise the temperature of the yolks slightly. Do this three more times until the yolks are warm enough to add the remainder of the grits. (Be careful not to add too much at once, which will cook and scramble the eggs.)

In a separate clean bowl, free of water drops or oil, whip the egg whites to smooth, stiff peaks with an electric beater. (They should be shiny white and able to stand up at the end of the beater.) With a large rubber spatula, gently fold one-third of the whites into the grits mixture to lighten the base. Do this twice more, taking care not to deflate the whites. Pour the mixture onto the prepared pan, spread it out evenly across the pan with the spatula, taking care not to deflate the egg whites, and immediately transfer to the oven. Bake for 15 minutes, or just until firm.

TO ASSEMBLE, remove the roulade from the oven. Place the second piece of buttered parchment on top and invert the roulade onto a large rack or cutting board. Peel the first piece of parchment off the roulade and discard. Layer the ham across the surface of the roulade and sprinkle with the 1 cup grated cheese, leaving a $^1/_2$-inch border. Starting with the long side of the roulade, roll it forward onto itself and continue doing so, pulling the parchment paper away from it as you progress, until you have a long cylinder.

Cut the roulade into 2-inch slices and serve immediately, or wrap the whole roulade in parchment and store in the refrigerator until ready to serve. The roulade keeps nicely up to 2 days. To reheat, place in a 325°F oven for 10 to 15 minutes, or until warm.

Grecian Frittata

Frittatas, or Italian omelets, have all of the versatility of their French counterparts without the fuss and fear of flipping. They are traditionally made in a skillet, and often started on the stovetop and finished off in the oven. These individual frittatas are baked in a muffin tin—excellent in a breakfast sandwich or for dinner with mixed greens and fresh fruit. Our version calls on Greek ingredients, but the recipe is so easy to customize, soon you'll be creating your own version based on whatever leftovers you have on hand. **Serves 4 to 6**

6 eggs

2 tablespoons whole milk

1 teaspoon kosher salt

$1/4$ teaspoon freshly ground black pepper

$1/2$ cup marinated artichoke hearts, chopped

$1/4$ cup pitted Kalamata olives (about 10 olives or 1.5 ounces), chopped

2 tablespoons finely chopped red onion

$1/2$ cup loosely packed spinach, chopped

$1/2$ cup crumbled feta cheese

Preheat the oven to 375°F. Coat 6 cups of a standard 12-cup muffin pan with butter or olive oil.

Whisk the eggs and milk together in a large bowl and season with the salt and pepper. In a small bowl, toss together the artichoke hearts, olives, red onion, spinach, and cheese.

Divide the vegetables and cheese among the coated muffin cups and pour whisked egg on top. Place the muffin pan on top of a rimmed baking sheet and transfer to the oven. Bake for 20 to 25 minutes, until the eggs are done to your liking. (Less time will yield moist, slightly runny frittatas. More baking will yield spongier, drier eggs.) Run a knife along the insides of each muffin cup to free any frittatas that may have baked onto the pan. Place a cutting board or a baking sheet on top of the muffin tin and invert the frittatas out of the pan. Serve immediately, or cool and refrigerate. To reheat later, place in a 325°F oven for 10 to 15 minutes, or until warm.

Chilaquiles

Traditional recipes for *chilaquiles* call for a mélange of ingredients simmered with dried and fried tortillas in red or green sauce. This version employs the same flavors in a different presentation. Eggs any style—poached, fried, sunny-side up, or scrambled—top off the crisp tortillas painted with deep red sauce. A drizzle of Mexican crema (or a dollop of sour cream) and a crumble of queso fresco round out the stacks for a delicious breakfast, brunch, lunch, or dinner. Feel free to toast the tortillas in a 375°F oven for 10 to 15 minutes if you'd rather not fry them. **Serves 4**

Red Sauce

1 (28-ounce) can whole peeled tomatoes, drained

1 medium jalapeño, seeded and coarsely chopped

1 small shallot, coarsely chopped

2 medium cloves garlic, coarsely chopped

1 tablespoon butter

$1\frac{1}{2}$ cups dried black beans, cooked, or 1 (15-ounce) can, drained and rinsed

Chilaquiles

1 cup vegetable oil

8 (6-inch) corn tortillas

Salt

4 to 8 eggs

1 cup crumbled queso fresco or Cotija cheese

$\frac{1}{2}$ cup crema or sour cream

TO MAKE THE SAUCE, put the tomatoes, jalapeño, shallot, and garlic in a blender and process until smooth. Heat the butter in a sauté pan over medium heat. Pour the blended mixture into the pan, stir in the black beans, and simmer the sauce for 15 minutes.

TO PREPARE THE CHILAQUILES, heat the oil to 350°F in a deep pot or Dutch oven. Gently lower one or two tortillas into the hot oil with a pair of metal tongs and fry for about 1 minute on each side, until golden. Remove from the oil and transfer to a cooling rack lined with paper towels. Sprinkle with salt. Repeat with the remaining tortillas.

Prepare the eggs to order for each serving (see headnote above). Place a tortilla on a plate, ladle about $\frac{1}{4}$ cup of the sauce on top, sprinkle with cheese, and add a dollop of crema. Stack a second tortilla on top of that layer, creating another in the same manner. Top with an egg and serve.

> **tip:** *No deep fry thermometer? You can determine the temperature of the oil by sticking the handle of a wooden spoon in the hot oil. If it's at just the right frying temperature, a steady stream of bubbles will come up from the handle. If it's not quite hot enough, just a few tiny bubbles will appear, whereas if the oil is too hot, it will spurt and sputter around the spoon.*

Pizza Strata

Essentially savory bread puddings, strata recipes can easily be adapted to use up leftovers or extend a few ingredients into a satisfying casserole capable of feeding a crowd. This version borrows the flavors of a pizza shop with a mix of classic toppings. As with most recipes, the outcome depends largely on the quality of your ingredients. We like Sicilian pepperoni and imported sharp provolone for this dish. **Serves 6 to 8**

1 (1-pound) loaf Italian bread, cut into 1-inch cubes

1 tablespoon olive oil

4 ounces pepperoni, cut into $1/4$-inch dice

2 shallots, minced

1 (10-ounce) package frozen spinach, defrosted and squeezed dry

1 clove garlic, minced

1 cup ricotta cheese

$1/4$ cup firmly packed fresh basil leaves, chopped

Salt and freshly ground black pepper

5 large eggs

$1^1/2$ cups whole milk

$3/4$ cup grated mozzarella cheese (about 3 ounces)

$3/4$ cup grated provolone cheese (about 3 ounces)

10 slow-roasted tomatoes (see page 52), coarsely chopped

Preheat the oven to 225°F. Butter a 9 by 13-inch baking dish.

Spread the bread cubes on a rimmed baking sheet, and bake for 10 minutes. Set aside.

TO PREPARE THE RICOTTA-SPINACH MIXTURE, heat the oil in a frying pan over medium heat for 1 minute. Add the pepperoni and shallots and sauté for 8 to 10 minutes, or until the shallot has softened and the pepperoni has rendered some of its fat. Add the spinach and sauté for another 2 to 3 minutes. In a small bowl, combine the spinach mixture with the garlic, ricotta, and basil. Taste the mixture for salt and adjust the seasoning. (This will depend a lot on your pepperoni.) Set aside.

In a bowl, whisk the eggs and milk together with a pinch of salt and pepper. Set aside. In another bowl, combine the cheeses.

TO ASSEMBLE THE STRATA, line the bottom of the prepared baking dish with one-third of the bread cubes. Dot with one-half of the ricotta-spinach mixture, one-half of the roasted tomatoes, and one-third of the cheeses. Layer another one-third of the bread cubes and top with the remaining spinach-ricotta mixture, the remaining tomatoes, and one-third of the cheeses. Layer the last one-third of the bread cubes and pour the egg and milk mixture evenly over the casserole. Press down with the back of a spatula. Top with the remaining one-third of the cheeses, and refrigerate at least one hour or overnight.

TO BAKE THE STRATA, preheat the oven to 350°F and bake for 45 minutes to 1 hour, until brown on top and a toothpick inserted in the middle comes out clean. Set on a wire rack to cool for at least 10 minutes before slicing.

tip: *Instead of toasting fresh bread, substitute any good quality day-old bread and skip the toasting.*

Flavorful Stocks and Broths

Stocks and broths are the basis of authentic, unprocessed flavor in soups, stews, sauces, and more.

A quietly gurgling pot of stock on the stovetop inspires nostalgia with aromas that evoke the idyllic comforts of home. But something so charmingly simple has the power to alter the entire flavor profile of a dish. Homemade stocks and broths are potions made from unadulterated foodstuffs including vegetables, herbs, spices, roasted bones, and hearty meats. Unlike many commercially made stocks packed in cans and boxes, homemade varieties are free of additives and flavor enhancers like MSG (see page 8), autolyzed yeast extract (see page 37), and boiling-over sodium levels. They are also virtually fat free. Their ability to enhance other ingredients comes from stock's mouth-filling flavors and smooth, velvety body, properties that develop over hours on the stove.

If your kitchen isn't as serene as the scene evoked by associated smells, the glory of stocks and broths is even more apparent. They require little prep and practically no attention but provide substance to dishes that's almost impossible to mimic. Plus, this liquid is some of the most freezer-friendly stuff in your kitchen. Freeze small batches (even in ice cube trays) so you have portions on hand to pop into sauces or make single servings of soup.

Collagen and gelatin provide the richness of homemade stocks and broths. Collagen is a connective tissue protein that dissolves in liquid, and gelatin is a mixture of proteins that thickens and stabilizes liquids. Meat and bones are rich in both. Collagen becomes jellylike in cold temperatures. If you've ever pulled out the leftover turkey from the fridge the day after Thanksgiving, you've been acquainted with gelatin, that Jello-ish stuff at the bottom of the roasting pan. These natural substances offer unbeatable and irreplaceable body to homemade soups and sauces made from reduced stock.

Bones and meat constitute the basic semantic difference between a stock and a broth. A stock is typically chock-full of bare bones from beef, pork, fish, or poultry. Broth usually extracts flavor from meat that is added to or used in lieu of bones. Both produce excellent results. While vegetable broth is meatless and boneless, fresh ingredients make an equally flavorful liquid. To boost body in your vegetable broths, add a peeled and quartered potato or two. The natural starches will help thicken the liquid, just as lentils do in our All-Purpose Vegetable Broth (page 137).

MAKING **STOCKS** AND **BROTHS**

Whether you're making a dark, intense roasted beef stock or a light, earthy vegetable broth, the principles and methods are the same.

Always start with just enough cold water to cover the surface of the topmost ingredients. Cold water coaxes impurities from the ingredients, which coagulate and rise to the surface as the water warms. Next, simmer the liquid gently. Boiling forces impurities and fat from the surface into the liquid, making it cloudy and greasy. The simmer time required depends on the type of stock. Beef bones need at least 8 hours to pull rich collagen and flavor from the bones. Poultry stocks are done in half that time, and fish and vegetable varieties come together in about an hour. Skim foam and fat from the surface several times throughout. Strain the liquid from the solids into a clean container immediately at the end of the simmer time to prevent the liquid from getting cloudy. Wait

to add salt and pepper to stocks and broths until you use them in recipes so the seasoning balances with the other ingredients. If you are not using the stock or broth right away, cool it to room temperature quickly. Dividing it into smaller containers will bring the temperature down faster. Alternatively, set the container of hot liquid on a stovetop grate in the kitchen sink. Fill the sink with cold water, about three-fourths of the way up the container. Once the liquid is cool enough, transfer it to storage containers, cover, and refrigerate. Any remaining fat will solidify on the top as it gets cold. Lift the fat away from the stock and discard it.

Most stocks and broths keep well in an air-tight container in the refrigerator for up to five days. The exception is fish stock, which should usually be used or frozen within two to three days. Stock and broth will keep well in the freezer for several months.

Basic Chicken Stock

This flavorful liquid makes a delicious supper with tiny pasta and a flurry of Parmesan cheese stirred in, along with a green salad on the side, but its homemade goodness will also transform a variety of more complex soups. Chicken stock is applicable to so many recipes it's always a good thing to have on hand. We think of it as liquid gold. If your stockpot is large enough, double the ingredients and freeze in smaller batches for multiple uses. **Makes about 8 cups**

1 tablespoon vegetable oil	1 bunch parsley
2 large yellow or white onions, quartered	6 sprigs thyme
3 medium carrots, cut into 3-inch chunks	1 bay leaf
3 large stalks celery, cut into 3-inch chunks	10 black peppercorns
3 cloves garlic, smashed and peeled	12 cups cold water
3 to 4 pounds bone-in, skin-on chicken pieces (whole wings are ideal)	

Heat the oil in a stockpot over medium-high heat. Add the onions, carrots, celery, and garlic and sauté for about 5 minutes. Place the chicken pieces on top of the vegetables and add the parsley, thyme, bay leaf, and peppercorns. Cover the ingredients with the water. Bring to a boil and immediately reduce the heat to a bare simmer. Continue cooking at a simmer for 3 to 4 hours, occasionally skimming the surface of foam and fat. Strain the liquid through a mesh strainer into a clean pot, discarding the solids. Use immediately, or cool and transfer to the refrigerator or freezer for later use.

SECRET **INGREDIENT**

One of our power players, Parmesan cheese, delivers on flavor right up to its very end—the rind. Add this last bit to the pot of ingredients simmering in stocks and broths destined for soup. The rind lends the cheese's trademark nutty and salty tastes to the liquid and puts a quality product to use.

Parmigiano-Reggiano is considered the best Parmesan cheese and is made only in Parma and the surrounding area in Italy. You can spot the real deal by its rind, which is etched with the words "Parmigiano-Reggiano" if it's authentic.

Roasted Turkey Stock

Turkey stock is the blissful destiny of lucky leftovers from Thanksgiving. If you start this recipe with holiday carvings and the entire remaining carcass, pick up the instructions below where the vegetables and turkey parts come together in the stockpot. If you are making this stock at any time other than the last week in November, here is a method that features classic turkey flavor in a liquid as adaptable as chicken stock to various recipes. Roasting the turkey parts first yields a brown stock. For a white stock, like the basic chicken stock, skip the roasting and proceed as noted. **Makes 14 cups**

3 pounds turkey parts (neck, drumstick, full wing)

1 medium yellow onion, cut into large chunks

2 large (8-ounce) carrots, cut into 1-inch pieces

3 stalks celery, cut into 1-inch pieces

3 cloves garlic, smashed

$1/3$ cup dry white wine

1 bay leaf

$1/4$ teaspoon black peppercorns (about 20)

1 bunch parsley (about $1/4$ cup)

5 quarts cold water

Preheat the oven to 475°F.

Place the turkey parts in a large roasting pan, and roast in the oven for about 1 hour, or until the turkey skin is nicely browned.

Transfer the turkey parts to a stockpot. Place the roasting pan over medium heat on the stovetop, add the onion, carrots, celery, and garlic, and sauté for about 5 minutes. Remove from the heat.

Move the vegetables to the stockpot. Deglaze the roasting pan with the wine, scraping the bottom. Pour the remnants into the stockpot with the turkey and vegetables. Add the bay leaf, peppercorns, parsley, and water. Bring the liquid to a boil and then immediately reduce the heat. Simmer for about 3 hours, skimming the foam from the surface occasionally.

Strain the liquid through a mesh strainer into a clean pot, discarding the solids. Use immediately, or cool and transfer to the refrigerator or freezer for later use.

STOCKING YOUR KITCHEN

You don't have to own fancy gadgets and equipment to make quality stocks and broths. These basics are all you really need.

Heavy-bottomed stockpot: This is the perfect vessel for the long simmer required to produce deeply flavored stocks and broths. Restaurants use pots upward of 60 quarts to churn out mass quantities, but an 8-quart pot will serve home cooks well. Ideally, your kitchen is stocked with two of the same size pot, or a large storage container, to strain the liquid into when it is done. Of course, bigger stockpots yield more in one shot. If you are dedicating a few hours to the recipe, and as long as there is enough room in your freezer, why not double the batch?

Mesh strainer: A small-holed colander will work for straining stocks and broth in a pinch, but a mesh strainer is better, and it's a minimal investment. Its tightly woven screen holds back big solids and miniscule bits from the flavorful liquid after hours of simmering. Opt for a wide basket with a metal lip that fits over the side of the clean pot or container you are straining into so that both hands are free to tilt the full stockpot. Don't feel obliged to buy restaurant gadgets like a China cap or chinois, which are expensive and difficult to store.

Wide, metal ladle: Use this for skimming foam and fat from the top of the liquid as it simmers. Doing so keeps the liquid clear and prevents it from having a greasy mouthfeel.

Cheesecloth and butcher string: Available in most grocery stores, these are used to tie up herbs and spices when making sachets and bouquets garnis to add to the simmering liquid. The little pouch (sachet) or bundle of herbs on a string is easy to pull out of the liquid when it is finished simmering.

Simple Fish Stock

Essential for seafood-based soups and stews like cioppino and bouillabaisse, fish stock is just as important to have on hand as the more commonly homemade chicken stock. Luckily, it's even easier to make. It requires just an hour on the stove for these simple ingredients to become a flavorful base for your dishes. If many of your favorite recipes are for seafood, you can easily double this amount and freeze it in 2-cup containers so you always have some ready to go. **Makes about 5 cups**

2 pounds fish bones or trimmings, well rinsed and cut into 3-inch pieces

1 small onion, coarsely chopped

2 medium carrots, coarsely chopped

1 stalk celery, coarsely chopped

6 parsley stems

$1/4$ lemon

10 black peppercorns

$2/3$ cup dry white wine

1 bay leaf

8 cups cold water

Put all the ingredients in a stockpot, bring the liquid to a boil, and immediately reduce the heat to low. Simmer for 1 hour, skimming any foam that comes to the surface. Strain the stock through a colander lined with cheesecloth, pressing to extract as much liquid as possible. Use within two days or freeze the stock for three months.

STOCK MARKET

When you're pressed for time and reaching for packaged broths and stocks, look for varieties that contain minimal amounts of additives, particularly unrecognizable ingredients. The lower sodium versions are also your best bet, both for the sake of nutrition and flavor. When the liquid simmers and reduces, added salt can make the results unpalatable. Better to opt for less salt to start and add more in the end if necessary. Homemade stocks really make an impact in some of the simplest recipes. In French Onion Soup (page 91), for example, luscious beef stock is more than just the backdrop to sweet, savory caramelized onions; it's collagen-richness lends viscosity and depth of flavor that commercial alternatives can't imitate. In other recipes, such as Lentil Soup (page 69), stock plays a supporting role with tons of other ingredients, so a quality boxed stock or broth will still yield delicious results.

Beef Stock

It's true that beef stock is an all-day affair, but usually so is cleaning your house. Both yield lasting benefits. Plus if your stockpot is big enough, you can freeze batches for a cold rainy day. Have the butcher cut the bones into pot-size chunks. It doesn't need your attention once it's simmering, so add it your agenda for house-cleaning day. **Makes 10 cups**

3 pounds beef bones

3 tablespoons tomato paste

2 medium onions, quartered

2 medium carrots, cut into 1-inch chunks

2 medium stalks celery, cut into 1-inch chunks

3 cloves garlic, smashed

$1/3$ cup dry red wine

10 sprigs parsley

10 sprigs thyme

10 black peppercorns

1 bay leaf

4 quarts cold water

Preheat the oven to 375°F.

Brush the bones all over with the tomato paste. Place in a roasting pan and roast for 1 hour. Move the roasting pan to the stove over medium-high heat. Transfer the bones to a stockpot and set aside. Add the onions, carrots, celery, and garlic to the roasting pan and sauté for about 15 minutes, just until they begin to brown. Pour in the wine, scraping the browned bits from the bottom and sides of the pan. Pour the liquid and vegetables into the stockpot with the bones, add the parsley, thyme, peppercorns, and bay leaf, and fill with the water. Bring the liquid to a boil and then drop the heat to medium-low. Simmer the stock for 8 hours, skimming occasionally.

Strain the liquid through a mesh strainer into a clean pot, discarding the solids. Use immediately, or cool and transfer to the refrigerator or freezer for later use.

Ham Stock

Baked ham usually means holiday guests and lots of leftovers. But just like the Thanksgiving turkey carcass, the odds and ends should be put to good use. After the last relative has gone, toss that spiral ham bone into a stockpot with veggies and water and let it simmer while you rest. The resulting stock, redolent with that trademark smoky aroma and flavor, is the perfect backdrop for hearty stews or gentler springtime soups. If you didn't start with a holiday ham, just swap in a few hocks or shanks, available at your butcher or most grocery stores. **Makes 14 cups**

2 teaspoons vegetable oil

2 medium onions, cut into 1-inch chunks

2 medium carrots, cut into 1-inch chunks

2 stalks celery, cut into 1-inch chunks

2 cloves garlic, smashed

1/4 cup dry white wine

2 to 3 pounds ham bones (shank, hock, or left over from spiral ham)

1 cup loosely packed parsley leaves (about 4 sprigs)

10 black peppercorns

1 sprig thyme

1 bay leaf

4 to 5 quarts cold water

Heat the oil in a stockpot over medium-high heat. Add the onions, carrots, celery, and garlic and cook, stirring occasionally, for about 5 to 7 minutes, or until the vegetables just begin to brown. Pour in the wine and scrape the bottom of the pan to release the browned bits. Add the bones and the parsley, peppercorns, thyme, bay leaf, and water. Bring the liquid to a boil, then drop the heat to medium and simmer for at least 2 hours. Strain the liquid through a mesh strainer into a clean pot, discarding the solids. Use immediately, or cool and transfer the stock to the refrigerator or freezer for later use.

All-Purpose Vegetable Broth

Vegetable stock is often the key to flavorful vegetarian dishes. This all-purpose version is easy to put together and much more flavorful than its supermarket counterpart. If you're making it for a specific dish, tailor it to your needs. Many vegetarian star ingredients, such as fennel or squash, make perfect additions to stock. Asparagus stems make an especially nice addition in the spring. In the chillier months, for caramelized, wintry flavors that will keep you warm, roast the vegetables in a 400°F oven for 30 minutes before simmering them. Ideally, stock making is a method you customize to your taste and repertoire of favorite meals. Nutritional yeast, available at health food stores, has a pleasant cheeselike flavor, which adds a little umami and a lot of B vitamins to this vegan brew. **Makes about 8 cups**

1 tablespoon olive oil

1 large onion, coarsely chopped

2 shallots, halved

3 carrots, halved lengthwise and chopped into 1-inch pieces

3 stalks celery, including leaves, chopped into 1-inch pieces

5 cloves garlic, smashed and peeled

1 1/2 tablespoons nutritional yeast

2 bay leaves

5 sprigs parsley

2 tablespoons green or black lentils

10 black peppercorns

12 cups cold water

1 stalk lemongrass

3 tablespoons tomato juice

Heat the oil in a large stockpot over medium-high heat. Add the onion, shallots, carrots, celery, and garlic. Cook for at least 10 minutes, allowing the vegetables to brown around the edges. After the vegetables have softened and browned slightly, add the yeast, bay leaves, and parsley. Stir to combine. Add the lentils, peppercorns, and water, scraping up any browned bits on the bottom of the pan, and bring to a boil. Reduce the heat to medium-low and simmer for 20 minutes. Add the lemongrass and tomato juice and simmer for another 10 minutes. Strain the liquid through a mesh strainer into a clean pot, discarding the solids. Use immediately, or cool and transfer to the refrigerator or freezer for later use.

Mushroom Broth

The earthy, hearty flavors of mushrooms make them an excellent candidate for a vegetable broth with robust flavor. Umami richness makes this broth ample enough to be a meat stock alternative. For added depth, toss the fresh mushrooms in a tablespoon of olive oil and roast them in a 375°F oven for 30 minutes before proceeding with the rest of the recipe. **Makes about 8 cups**

2 teaspoons olive oil

1 medium onion, coarsely chopped

1 medium carrot, cut into $\frac{1}{4}$-inch dice ($\frac{1}{2}$ cup)

1 stalk celery, cut into $\frac{1}{4}$-inch dice (about $\frac{1}{4}$ cup)

4 scallions, white and green parts, chopped into 1-inch pieces

3 cloves garlic, peeled and smashed

1 pound mixed fresh mushrooms (such as white button, cremini, and shiitake), halved

$\frac{1}{2}$ ounce (about $\frac{1}{3}$ cup) dried porcini mushrooms

$\frac{1}{4}$ cup dry white wine

10 black peppercorns

1 bunch parsley

5 fresh sage leaves

3 sprigs thyme

10 cups cold water

2 tablespoons soy sauce

1 tablespoon sherry vinegar

Heat the olive oil in a large stockpot over medium-high heat. Add the onion, carrot, and celery and sauté for 5 minutes. Mix in the scallions, garlic, and the fresh mushrooms, cooking for another 5 minutes, until the mushrooms start to soften and become fragrant. Add the porcini and wine and let simmer for 2 minutes. Add the peppercorns, parsley, sage, thyme, and water. Bring the liquid to a boil and then drop the heat to a bare simmer. Let the broth simmer for 1 hour, skimming the foam from the top occasionally.

Remove the broth from the heat and strain it into a clean pot, discarding the solids. Add the soy sauce and vinegar. Use immediately, or cool and transfer to the refrigerator or freezer for later use.

resources

BOOKS

In the process of writing this cookbook, we pored over countless volumes that went before ours. Here is an abbreviated list of those we relied on most heavily. They are recommended reads for anyone interested in becoming a good home cook.

Bayless, Rick. *Authentic Mexican: Regional Cooking from the Heart of Mexico*. With Deann Groen Bayless. New York: Morrow, 2007.

Beard, James. *The New James Beard*. New York: Knopf, 1981.

Child, Julia, Louisette Bertholle, and Simone Beck. *Mastering the Art of French Cooking*. New York: Knopf, 2004.

Corriher, Shirley O. *Cookwise*. New York: Morrow, 1997.

Drummand, Karen Eich, and Lisa M. Brefere. *Nutrition for Foodservice & Culinary Professionals*. 5th ed. Hoboken, NJ: Wiley, 2004.

Green, Aliza. *Beans*. Philadelphia: Running Press, 2004.

———. *Starting with Ingredients*. Philadelphia: Running Press, 2006.

Herbst, Sharon Tyler. *The New Food Lover's Companion*. 3rd ed. Hauppauge, NY: Barron's, 2001.

Jaffrey, Madhur. *Indian Cooking*. Hauppauge, NY: Barron's, 2002.

Jenkins, Steve. *The Cheese Primer*. New York: Workman, 1996.

Joachim, David. *The Food Substitutions Bible*. Toronto: Robert Rose, 2005.

Kingsolver, Barbara. *Animal, Vegetable, Miracle: A Year of Food Life*. With Steven L. Hopp and Camille Kingsolver. New York: HarperCollins, 2007.

Labensky, Sarah R., and Alan M. Hause. *On Cooking: A Textbook of Culinary Fundamentals*. 3rd ed. Upper Saddle River, NJ: Prentice Hall, 2003.

Madison, Deborah. *Vegetarian Cooking for Everyone*. New York: Broadway Books, 1997.

McCalman, Max, and David Gibbons. *Cheese: A Connoisseur's Guide to the World's Best*. New York: Clarkson Potter, 2005.

McDermott, Nancy. *Quick & Easy Thai*. San Francisco: Chronicle Books, 2004.

McGee, Harold. *On Food and Cooking: The Science and Lore of the Kitchen*. New York: Scribner, 2004.

Peterson, James. *Splendid Soups*. New York: Bantam, 1993.

Pollan, Michael. *In Defense of Food: An Eater's Manifesto*. New York: Penguin, 2008.

———. *The Omnivore's Dilemma: A Natural History of Four Meals*. New York: Penguin, 2006.

Schloss, Andrew, and David Joachim. *Mastering the Grill: The Owner's Manual for Outdoor Cooking*. San Francisco: Chronicle Books, 2007.

Simmons, Marie. *The Good Egg: More than 200 Fresh Approaches from Soup to Dessert*. Boston: Houghton Mifflin, 2000.

Weinstein, Bruce, and Mark Scarbrough. *The Ultimate Potato Book: Hundreds of Ways to Turn America's Favorite Side Dish into a Meal*. New York: Morrow, 2003.

Yin, Ellen. *Forklore*. Philadelphia: Temple University Press, 2007.

WEB SITES

Much of the public discussion about the issues that have informed this book happens online. The following sites offer serious news items, information about where to find the kind of products mentioned in our recipes, active communities of like-minded people who consider sustainable food an urgent issue, and entertainment.

American Grassfed Association
www.americangrassfed.org

Blue Ocean Institute
www.blueocean.org

Eat Wild
www.eatwild.com

Food Routes
www.foodroutes.org

King Corn
www.kingcorn.net

Local Harvest
www.localharvest.org

The Meatrix
www.themeatrix.com

Penzeys Spices
www.penzeys.com

Salmon Nation
www.salmonnation.com

Serious Eats
www.seriouseats.com

Slow Food
www.slowfoodusa.org

Sustainable Table
www.sustainabletable.org

Truth in Labeling
www.truthinlabeling.org

USDA
www.usda.gov

index